CAUSAL INFERENCE IN THE WILD

Unlocking Cause and Effect in Observational Data Studies

Austine Unuriode

Table Of Contents

Preface

This book was written with the aim of making sense of one of the most elusive yet powerful challenges in science, business, and human decision-making, the quest to truly understand cause and effect. For centuries people have asked questions about why things happen, but with the advancement of data collection and the explosion of information in the digital era, the opportunity to answer these questions has taken on new urgency. However, unlike the controlled environment of randomized experiments, most of the data we deal with in reality comes from the messiness of the world itself. These are observational data, streams of information not created under the neat structure of scientific trials but generated as people act, as systems interact, and as environments evolve. To navigate this, causal inference has emerged as the bridge between correlation and truth. This book is not intended for a narrow group of academic researchers alone. It is written for data scientists, analysts, policy makers, business leaders, and anyone who needs to make decisions with imperfect but abundant information. It is meant to give you not just tools, but also an understanding of the reasoning behind those tools, the principles that make causal inference reliable when used carefully, and the pitfalls that await when it is misapplied. I want readers to leave with clarity, confidence, and a sense of possibility in their ability to reason about causality even in the wild chaos of real-world data. This book was born out of a deep recognition that in our data-driven age, answers are too often mistaken for truths, and patterns are too easily celebrated as causal discoveries without the rigor they demand. As a data scientist I have observed firsthand how organizations, researchers, and policymakers cling to correlations with the hope that they reveal more than they actually do, only to later discover that decisions made on these fragile foundations can collapse when tested against the realities of causation. My motivation in writing this work is not only to illuminate the methods that allow us to move beyond association but also to cultivate a mindset in readers that is both critical and courageous when approaching the complexity of observational data. Unlike experiments that are neatly controlled and designed for causal clarity, the real world rarely affords us such simplicity. Data collected from the messy interactions of human behavior, economic exchange, environmental change, and technological adoption contain within them both immense insight and deceptive noise. Navigating these complexities is not about searching for a perfect formula but about learning to reason with discipline, humility, and methodological creativity. This is the philosophy that underpins every chapter of this book. I want readers to see causal inference not as a set of statistical tricks to impress colleagues but as a framework for thinking that sharpens decision making, enriches understanding, and challenges assumptions that might otherwise go unquestioned. The journey through this book mirrors the journey of data itself. We begin with confusion, where relationships seem to appear out of nowhere and suggest truths that feel convincing. Then we confront skepticism, realizing that confounders, biases, and unmeasured variables can lead us astray. From there we embrace structure, employing models, frameworks, and assumptions that allow us to separate what is plausible from what is speculative. Finally, we arrive at interpretation, where the goal is not only to compute estimates of causal effect but also to understand the limits of what we can claim and the responsibility attached to those claims. In writing this book I have been influenced by pioneers in statistics, econometrics, computer science, and philosophy who have shown that cause and effect is not a luxury of randomized experiments but a pursuit that can be meaningfully undertaken even when randomness is absent. Yet while their contributions form the foundation, I have chosen to write not for specialists alone but for anyone who grapples with the question of why things happen as they do and who must act on those answers in practical settings. Whether you are a researcher navigating complex social data, a policymaker confronted with urgent decisions, a business leader seeking to understand consumer behavior, or a student eager to sharpen your analytical toolkit, this book is designed to meet you where you are while challenging you to reach higher. It will not oversimplify the field, but it will strive to keep concepts intelligible, to emphasize intuition alongside mathematics, and to provide real-world illustrations that anchor abstract ideas in concrete reality. Writing a book like this also means confronting the limits of certainty.

Causal inference in observational studies will never yield perfect answers. The goal is not perfection but progress, not finality but refinement, and not authority but clarity. This is why I have emphasized both the potential and the pitfalls throughout these pages, ensuring that readers walk away with a balanced appreciation for the power of causal inference as well as a respect for its boundaries. The title of this book, Causal Inference in the Wild, reflects my conviction that the real practice of causal reasoning does not take place in tidy laboratories but in the unpredictable, noisy, and high-stakes environments where data is generated without our control. It is in these settings that the need for rigor is greatest and the temptation to settle for easy answers is strongest. To succeed in the wild we must carry with us tools, strategies, and a disciplined way of thinking that keeps us grounded in evidence while open to complexity. Above all, this book is a call to intellectual honesty. In the rush to extract value from data, it is easy to forget that every number represents part of a story, every model carries assumptions, and every inference has consequences for real people and institutions. The challenge of causal inference is not just technical but ethical, requiring us to weigh the cost of error, the risk of bias, and the significance of the conclusions we share. As you embark on this journey through the chapters ahead, I invite you to keep both the ambition of discovery and the humility of uncertainty alive in your mind. Let this book serve as a guide, not a rulebook, and as an encouragement to approach causal inference not as a finished science but as a living practice that evolves with data, context, and inquiry. My hope is that when you finish reading these pages, you will not only know how to unlock cause and effect in observational data but also feel inspired to approach the world with deeper curiosity, greater rigor, and a sharper sense of responsibility.

Foreword

When I was first introduced to causal inference, it seemed like an abstract exercise filled with complex mathematics, assumptions, and unfamiliar terminology. It felt distant from the pressing problems of health, economics, and technology that I saw in the world. Yet as I went deeper, I realized that causal inference is not merely an academic pursuit but one of the most practical and transformative skills one can develop. The ability to distinguish what is truly causing an outcome from what is merely associated with it has consequences that ripple across every decision we make as societies and individuals. Without causal reasoning, we risk mistaking signals for truths, pouring resources into ineffective policies, or drawing conclusions that do more harm than good. This book captures that realization and translates it into a structured journey that is accessible, rigorous, and profoundly relevant. The author has succeeded in presenting causal inference not as a dry theoretical domain but as a living discipline shaped by real problems and real data. The chapters take the reader from the foundations of causality into the practical applications that confront researchers, companies, and governments every day. By reading this book, you are not simply learning a set of techniques, you are stepping into a way of thinking that has the power to reshape how you view problems, interpret information, and act upon evidence. The book does not oversimplify, nor does it assume that the reader must be an advanced statistician to understand. It provides depth without alienation, precision without obscurity, and application without compromise. As you move through its pages, I encourage you to approach it not just as a technical manual but as a conversation with one of the most fundamental questions of knowledge: what is the true relationship between cause and effect.

Introduction

Causality is at the heart of human curiosity. From the earliest observations of nature to the most sophisticated analyses of modern science, we have always sought to answer the question of why something happens. If we see a pattern in the world, we instinctively want to know whether one event brought about another or whether the two simply happened together by coincidence. This is more than a philosophical exercise. It defines how we treat disease, how we design policy, how we run businesses, and how we build technology. The difficulty, however, is that while correlation is easy to observe, causation is difficult to prove. The problem of inferring cause from effect has been with humanity since the dawn of reason, and even today, with vast amounts of data at our disposal, the challenge remains. Most data do not come from controlled experiments where researchers can carefully assign treatments and track outcomes under identical conditions. Instead, most data are observational, arising from the uncontrolled, dynamic interactions of people, markets, and environments. Observational data are messy, biased, and incomplete. Yet they are also abundant and often the only kind available. To understand how smoking affects health, how economic policies affect poverty, or how product designs affect consumer behavior, we must rely on the evidence produced by real-world data. This is where causal inference steps in as a discipline that blends statistical methods, logical reasoning, and domain knowledge to approximate the answers that experiments might have provided, if only they were possible. To appreciate the significance of causal inference in observational studies, one must first understand the limitations of traditional statistics. When a correlation is observed, it only means that two variables move together. For example, ice cream sales may rise at the same time as drowning incidents. But does buying ice cream cause drowning. The more plausible explanation is that both are driven by a third factor, the hot weather. This simple example illustrates a deeper truth: without understanding causal structure, one risks drawing false conclusions. Traditional regression models may measure associations, but they cannot by themselves tell us whether one variable truly influences another. Causal inference, by contrast, seeks to untangle the web of relationships, identify confounders, and answer counterfactual questions such as what would have happened if things had been different. The counterfactual framework, pioneered by scholars like Donald Rubin and extended by Judea Pearl through causal graphs, provides a formal way of reasoning about such questions. The introduction of counterfactual reasoning allows us to ask questions beyond the data we observe. For instance, we may ask, what would have happened to a patient if they had not taken a drug, even though in reality they did. Such questions cannot be answered by correlations alone, but they can be approached through methods that attempt to simulate the missing world. Matching techniques, for example, try to create comparisons between treated and untreated groups that resemble an experiment. Instrumental variable methods attempt to exploit natural sources of variation that mimic random assignment. Difference in differences methods examine changes over time across groups that experience interventions at different points. Regression discontinuity designs use thresholds as quasi-random cutoffs. Each of these tools is imperfect, yet each is powerful when applied with care and when assumptions are clearly understood.The real challenge comes in applying these methods to observational data in the wild. Unlike controlled environments, the wild is filled with unobserved confounders, selection biases, measurement errors, and complex interactions. Data from hospitals may suffer from missing information. Data from online platforms may reflect the biases of user behavior. Data from economic systems may be shaped by countless unseen forces. The art of causal inference lies in navigating these imperfections without losing sight of rigor. This requires not only technical skill but also domain expertise, critical thinking, and a willingness to question assumptions. It is easy to run statistical models, but it is much harder to justify that the assumptions behind them hold in reality. This is why causal inference is not just a set of techniques but a way of thinking that demands skepticism, creativity, and responsibility. Why does this matter so much today. In the modern world, data-driven decision-making has become the norm. Governments rely on data to design policies, businesses rely on data to guide strategies, and individuals rely on data to make personal choices. Yet if these decisions are based on mere associations rather than causal understanding, the consequences can be harmful. A company may believe that increasing advertising spending always increases sales when in fact both may be driven by seasonal demand. A government may believe that increasing police presence reduces crime when in fact it merely changes reporting patterns. A hospital may believe that certain treatments save lives when in fact the patients receiving them were healthier to begin with. Misinterpreting correlation as causation can waste resources, misguide strategies, and even cost lives. By contrast, robust causal inference can lead to more effective policies, smarter business strategies, and better health outcomes. The importance of causal inference is not confined to traditional research. In the era of artificial intelligence and machine learning, models are increasingly used to predict outcomes and automate decisions. Yet predictive accuracy is not the same as causal understanding. A machine learning model may accurately predict who will default on a loan, but without causal reasoning, it cannot tell us whether changing an interest rate will reduce defaults. Similarly, a predictive model may forecast hospital admissions, but without causality, it cannot tell us whether a new intervention will actually reduce admissions. As AI systems become more integrated into society, the need to embed causal inference into their design becomes urgent. Otherwise, we risk building systems that are accurate but not useful, powerful but not responsible.

Throughout this book, we will explore both the principles and the practices of causal inference in observational data studies. We will begin with the conceptual foundations, examining what causality means, how it differs from correlation, and how philosophers and scientists have grappled with the concept over time. We will then move into the frameworks of counterfactuals and causal diagrams, which provide the formal backbone of modern causal reasoning. From there, we will dive into the methods available for extracting causal insights from observational data, explaining how each works, where it is most applicable, and what assumptions underlie it. Along the way, we will examine applications in diverse fields, from medicine to economics to technology. Finally, we will look at the challenges and future directions, considering how causal inference can evolve to meet the demands of increasingly complex and data-rich environments. As you engage with these ideas, it is important to remember that causal inference is not about perfection but about progress. No method can eliminate uncertainty entirely, but good methods can reduce it and guide decisions in a direction that is more reliable. The goal is not to achieve certainty but to achieve clarity, to move from blind association to informed judgment. This requires humility, because assumptions may fail, data may mislead, and conclusions may need revision. But it also requires courage, because without causal reasoning, we are left at the mercy of coincidence.

This book does not promise shortcuts, nor does it pretend that causality can be unlocked without effort. What it offers is a structured path, a set of tools, and a perspective that can help you approach the complexity of real-world data with rigor and confidence. Whether you are analyzing health records, economic trends, user behavior, or social policies, the principles of causal inference can transform the way you interpret information and make decisions. In a world where data are abundant but truth is elusive, the ability to reason about cause and effect is one of the most valuable skills you can develop. By the end of this book, I hope you will not only understand causal inference in theory but also appreciate its power in practice, and most importantly, feel equipped to use it wisely in the wild.

Chapter One

The Nature of Causality and Human Curiosity

From the earliest stages of human thought, the need to distinguish cause from coincidence has been fundamental. When ancient people observed the sun rising after the crowing of a rooster, the temptation was to assume that one caused the other. When they saw illness following the consumption of certain foods, they inferred that the food was responsible. When they noticed prosperity following the worship of particular gods, they assumed divine favor was the cause. These primitive interpretations reveal something deep about the human mind: the urge to seek causal connections is instinctive. Yet instinct can mislead. Just because two events follow each other in sequence does not mean one causes the other. To truly understand causality, humans had to move beyond observation to reasoning, beyond simple correlations to mechanisms, beyond superstition to systematic inquiry. The nature of causality is more than a pattern, it is the hidden structure that underlies why patterns occur. It represents the difference between prediction and understanding. A gambler might predict that a coin toss yields heads with a fifty percent chance, but understanding causality means recognizing that the design of the coin, the mechanics of the flip, and the absence of external manipulation create that probability. The same distinction applies in every domain of life. Doctors must distinguish between symptoms and causes, economists must separate market trends from underlying drivers, and scientists must parse natural phenomena into true chains of influence rather than coincidental co-occurrences. At its core, causality is about counterfactuals: asking what would have happened if things had been different. If a patient recovers after taking medicine, the causal question is whether they would have recovered without it. If a policy reduces unemployment, the causal question is whether unemployment would have declined anyway. This counterfactual perspective is essential, because it forces us to consider not only what we observe but also what we cannot directly see. Human curiosity naturally gravitates toward such questions. We are not content with merely knowing that two events are linked, we want to know whether one event could be controlled to produce the other. This is why causality is inherently tied to intervention. To say that smoking causes cancer is not merely to observe an association, it is to assert that reducing smoking would reduce cancer incidence. To say that education increases earnings is not merely to observe that educated people earn more, it is to assert that increasing education would raise incomes. The idea of causality therefore carries with it the possibility of change, agency, and control, making it not only a scientific concept but also a practical one. The nature of causality has been debated for centuries by philosophers and scientists alike. Aristotle distinguished four types of causes: material, formal, efficient, and final. David Hume argued that causality is nothing more than the habit of observing constant conjunctions, leading him to skepticism about whether we can ever truly know cause. Immanuel Kant countered that causality is a necessary category of human understanding, built into the very framework of how we perceive the world. In modern times, scientists such as Ronald Fisher, Donald Rubin, and Judea Pearl have developed mathematical frameworks that formalize these age-old debates into practical tools. Despite this intellectual progress, the central mystery remains: causality cannot be observed directly. We cannot step into parallel worlds to see both outcomes at once. We can only infer causality through reasoning, assumptions, and approximations. This is why causal inference is both powerful and limited. It is powerful because it allows us to reach beyond the data to insights about how the world works. It is limited because every inference rests on assumptions, and assumptions can be wrong. The nature of causality is thus not only an intellectual pursuit but also a moral one. To claim that one thing causes another is to make a statement with practical consequences. If we are wrong, people may suffer, resources may be wasted, or policies may fail. If we are right, lives may be improved, economies strengthened, and societies advanced. Human curiosity about causality is therefore inseparable from human responsibility. As we proceed deeper into the study of causal inference, this duality must remain clear: we seek not only to satisfy curiosity but also to guide action with care.

Correlation and Its Limitations in Observational Data

The distinction between correlation and causation has become one of the most repeated cautions in science and statistics. Yet despite its familiarity, the mistake of conflating the two remains one of the most common and costly errors in research, policy, and business. Correlation simply measures the degree to which two variables move together. If one increases when the other increases, the correlation is positive. If one increases when the other decreases, the correlation is negative. Correlation is useful for prediction but not sufficient for understanding. The classic example is the correlation between ice cream sales and drowning incidents. Both rise during the summer months, but it would be absurd to claim that buying ice cream causes drowning. The lurking factor is temperature, which increases both swimming activity and ice cream consumption. This illustrates confounding, where a third variable drives both the supposed cause and the supposed effect. In observational data, confounding is rampant. Consider health studies. People who exercise more may also eat healthier, smoke less, and have higher incomes. If researchers observe lower disease rates among those who exercise, exercise is the true cause, or is it income, diet, or smoking habits. Without controlling for confounders, conclusions risk being misleading. Another limitation of correlation is reverse causation. Suppose data show that higher stress levels are correlated with higher coffee consumption. One might conclude that coffee increases stress. Yet it may be the opposite: stressed people drink more coffee. Reverse causation is especially problematic in observational studies where temporal ordering is not always clear. Correlation also suffers from the problem of spurious relationships. With large datasets, it is possible to find correlations between completely unrelated variables, such as per capita cheese consumption and deaths by bedsheet entanglement. These relationships arise by chance and reveal nothing about the real world. In the age of big data, where millions of variables can be analyzed simultaneously, spurious correlations proliferate, making it even more essential to distinguish statistical artifacts from genuine causal mechanisms. The limitations of correlation highlight why observational data are challenging. In experimental settings, researchers can manipulate treatments and randomize assignments, ensuring that confounders are balanced across groups. This allows clear causal interpretations. In observational studies, by contrast, treatments are not assigned randomly but self-selected or naturally occurring. Smokers choose to smoke, wealthier students choose certain schools, companies choose where to invest. These choices are influenced by underlying factors that also affect outcomes, creating entanglements that correlation alone cannot resolve. This does not mean correlation is useless. Correlations can guide hypotheses, highlight potential relationships, and support predictions. In many fields, correlation-based models have practical value. For example, meteorologists use correlations between atmospheric variables to predict weather. Retailers use correlations between purchases to recommend products. But when the goal is to understand cause, correlation is insufficient. A policymaker cannot rely on correlation to decide whether increasing the minimum wage will reduce poverty. A doctor cannot rely on correlation to decide whether a new treatment will save lives. A business cannot rely on correlation to decide whether advertising truly drives sales. The cost of mistaking correlation for causation can be enormous. This is why causal inference has developed as a discipline distinct from correlation analysis. It acknowledges that observational data are riddled with confounding, reverse causation, and spurious relationships, and it seeks methods to overcome these problems. Tools such as propensity score matching, instrumental variables, and difference in differences are designed specifically to extract causal signals from noisy observational data. Each method carries assumptions, but each represents a step beyond mere correlation. Ultimately, the limitations of correlation remind us of a fundamental principle: patterns in data are not explanations. They are clues, not conclusions. They invite deeper inquiry but do not by themselves justify action. Recognizing this limitation is the first step toward responsible use of data in decision-making.

The Emergence of Causal Inference as a Scientific Discipline

Causal inference did not appear fully formed. It emerged gradually through centuries of philosophical debate, statistical innovation, and practical necessity. In the seventeenth century, philosophers such as Francis Bacon advocated systematic observation and experimentation as a way to uncover causal relationships. The scientific revolution institutionalized experiments as the gold standard for identifying causes. In medicine, pioneers such as James Lind conducted early randomized trials, like his famous experiment on scurvy among sailors. Yet even as experiments proved powerful, they were not always possible. Ethical, practical, and financial constraints limited their use. This created a demand for alternative methods that could extract causal insights from observational data. The twentieth century marked a turning point. Ronald Fisher developed the randomized controlled trial as a formal methodology, cementing experimentation as the cornerstone of causal research. At the same time, statisticians began developing tools to deal with observational data. The potential outcomes framework, introduced by Jerzy Neyman and later expanded by Donald Rubin, provided a mathematical structure for causal inference. It framed causality in terms of counterfactuals: what would happen to the same unit under different treatments. This framework made explicit the fundamental problem of causal inference, that we can never observe both outcomes for the same unit at the same time, and thus must rely on assumptions and methods to approximate them. In parallel, economists developed instrumental variable techniques to address confounding when natural experiments provided exogenous sources of variation. For example, the draft lottery in the United States served as an instrument for studying the effects of military service on life outcomes. Social scientists pioneered difference in differences approaches, using policy changes as natural experiments to compare treated and untreated groups over time. Regression discontinuity designs emerged as another quasi-experimental tool, exploiting thresholds such as test scores or income cutoffs to approximate randomization. In recent decades, Judea Pearl and colleagues advanced the graphical approach to causality, formalizing causal relationships as directed acyclic graphs. This framework allowed researchers to visualize assumptions, identify confounding structures, and determine whether causal effects could be estimated from available data. Pearl's do-calculus extended the language of probability into a language of intervention, making it possible to formally distinguish between correlation and causation. The emergence of causal inference as a scientific discipline reflects both intellectual progress and societal need. As data have become more abundant, the limitations of purely correlational analysis have become more apparent. Governments need to know whether policies cause change, not just whether they correlate with outcomes. Businesses need to know whether marketing campaigns drive sales, not just whether they are associated with them. Health researchers need to know whether treatments save lives, not just whether patients who take them survive. The rise of machine learning and artificial intelligence has only sharpened this demand. Predictive models may achieve high accuracy, but without causal inference, their predictions cannot guide interventions. If an algorithm predicts which patients are likely to be readmitted to the hospital, the key question is what actions can reduce readmission. Prediction alone cannot answer this, but causal inference can. The discipline of causal inference is thus not an academic curiosity but a response to practical challenges across fields as diverse as medicine, economics, education, technology, and public policy. Its methods are designed to make the best use of imperfect data, to approximate the insights of experiments when experiments are not feasible, and to provide a framework for reasoning under uncertainty. As a scientific discipline, causal inference is still evolving. New methods are being developed to handle high-dimensional data, complex interactions, and dynamic systems. Advances in computational power allow for sophisticated simulations and sensitivity analyses. Integration with machine learning is creating hybrid approaches that combine predictive accuracy with causal interpretability. The field is expanding not only in methods but also in scope, influencing disciplines from epidemiology to marketing to artificial intelligence. Yet amid this growth, the core principles remain unchanged: causality requires assumptions, those assumptions must be explicit, and conclusions must be tempered with humility. The emergence of causal inference reflects humanity's enduring quest to understand the forces that shape the world. It is a discipline born of necessity, nurtured by philosophy, and matured by science. It provides tools to navigate the complexities of observational data while respecting the limitations of knowledge. In this sense, causal inference is both ancient and modern, carrying forward the age-old human pursuit of why while equipping us to face the challenges of a data-rich but causally uncertain world.

Chapter Two

Principles of Study Design in Observational Research

Observational studies sit at the core of causal inference because in reality many questions cannot be investigated using randomized controlled trials and yet the pursuit of causality remains essential for advancing knowledge. The design of such studies is therefore the first and perhaps most critical step in ensuring that valid inferences can be made. Unlike randomized experiments where treatment allocation is under the direct control of the researcher, observational data arises from naturalistic environments where subjects select themselves into treatments or are exposed to conditions outside of experimental manipulation. This difference brings about challenges of confounding, selection bias, and missing data but also provides an opportunity to harness large scale data from real world sources such as administrative records, medical registries, digital platforms, or social environments. A properly designed observational study begins with clear articulation of the causal question. Without a precise question, all subsequent steps risk drifting into mere correlation seeking. The question must define the treatment or exposure, the target population, the outcome of interest, and the causal contrast being estimated. Once these elements are fixed, the researcher must carefully decide on the scope of data to be collected, the period of observation, and the units of analysis. Unlike simple descriptive analysis, causal study design requires anticipating sources of confounding and bias and strategizing about how to control them through design before resorting to analysis techniques. This is why the principle of comparability becomes central. Since subjects are not randomized into exposure groups, one must seek ways to approximate the counterfactual condition by assembling groups that are as similar as possible except for the treatment. Approaches such as restriction, matching, stratification, or constructing comparable cohorts are part of design level solutions that reduce bias before modeling begins. Each of these approaches carries assumptions and limitations that must be carefully weighed against the data generating process. Restriction involves limiting the sample to units with similar covariates in order to eliminate sources of variation that might confound the treatment effect. Matching attempts to pair treated and untreated units with similar background characteristics to approximate balance. Stratification divides the population into subgroups within which the treatment assignment is more comparable. These approaches are powerful in aligning groups but can reduce sample size or create difficulties when covariates are high dimensional. In addition to comparability, time ordering is a crucial principle. Treatment or exposure must precede outcome in a well-defined temporal sequence otherwise claims of causality collapse into ambiguity. Observational studies must therefore ensure that measurements of exposure and outcomes are collected in a way that preserves this ordering. Retrospective studies where data is reconstructed from existing records often struggle with this issue and require careful validation of timestamps and event ordering. Prospective designs, although more expensive, provide better control over temporal order. Another principle is clarity about the population of inference. Observational studies often arise from convenience samples, electronic records, or cohorts that may not represent the target population of interest. If generalizability is a goal, the design must explicitly consider representativeness or at least acknowledge limitations in external validity. This principle is tied to sampling strategies, inclusion and exclusion criteria, and data collection protocols that avoid systematic biases. Measurement validity also deserves attention at the design stage. Unlike experiments where variables can often be measured under standardized conditions, observational studies rely on existing records, self-reports, or environmental data streams where misclassification is common. Exposure misclassification, outcome misclassification, and measurement error in confounders can each bias causal estimates. Good design requires anticipating these sources and where possible incorporating validation studies, triangulation from multiple sources, or statistical adjustment strategies. Finally, ethical principles must govern observational study design. Even though interventions are not assigned by the researcher, the use of personal data, medical records, or sensitive information requires strict adherence to ethical review and protection of subjects. Transparency in objectives, secure data handling, and clear communication of risks are central to ethically sound research. By respecting these principles, observational studies become more than descriptive exercises and stand as rigorous vehicles for uncovering causal relationships in settings where experiments are impractical. A poorly designed observational study cannot be rescued by even the most sophisticated statistical modeling because flaws in design embed biases that cannot be removed post hoc. Therefore, the art of causal inference in observational settings begins with design grounded in principles of comparability, time ordering, validity, representativeness, and ethics. These design principles shape the credibility of every conclusion drawn from the data.

Strategies for Reducing Confounding and Bias at the Design Stage

Confounding is the primary enemy of causal inference in observational studies because it creates spurious associations between treatment and outcome that do not reflect causal effects.

The problem arises when a third variable influences both treatment assignment and the outcome, thereby distorting the observed relationship. For instance, in studying the effect of exercise on cardiovascular health, socioeconomic status could act as a confounder if it influences both likelihood of engaging in exercise and access to healthcare. Without adjusting for it, the causal estimate would be biased. Strategies to address confounding must therefore be integrated into the design of the study before data analysis. One fundamental strategy is careful selection of variables to measure. Unlike in simple predictive modeling where inclusion of any variable that improves prediction may be acceptable, causal inference requires deliberate inclusion of variables that capture common causes of treatment and outcome. This principle is guided by causal diagrams or directed acyclic graphs which provide a structured way of identifying potential confounders based on domain knowledge. Failure to measure and include key confounders leads to omitted variable bias which no amount of post hoc modeling can fix. Another strategy is matching. By pairing treated and untreated units that are similar in observed characteristics, researchers attempt to mimic the comparability of randomized experiments. Propensity score matching has become a popular implementation where the probability of receiving treatment given covariates is estimated and units are matched based on this score. The goal is to create balanced groups such that the distribution of observed covariates is similar across treatment statuses. Matching reduces bias from observed confounders but cannot address unmeasured ones. Stratification is another design stage approach. The sample is divided into homogeneous strata based on confounding variables and treatment effects are estimated within strata before being aggregated. This ensures that comparisons are made within comparable groups and reduces the influence of confounders. However stratification becomes unwieldy with many confounders. Restriction offers another avenue by limiting the sample to units within a narrow range of the confounding variable. For example, in a study of alcohol consumption and liver disease one might restrict the sample to non-smokers to eliminate smoking as a confounder. This approach simplifies analysis but at the cost of generalizability. Instrumental variable design is a more advanced strategy where an external variable influences treatment assignment but not the outcome except through treatment. By leveraging such instruments researchers can approximate randomization and reduce confounding. However finding valid instruments is often difficult and requires deep substantive knowledge. Sensitivity analysis should also be planned at the design stage to evaluate how robust findings are to potential unmeasured confounding. Bias beyond confounding must also be confronted. Selection bias occurs when the process of selecting subjects into the study is related to both treatment and outcome. For instance using only hospital data to study disease prevalence may bias results because hospitalized patients differ systematically from the general population. To mitigate this, careful attention to sampling frames and inclusion criteria is necessary. Information bias is another threat arising from misclassification of exposures, outcomes, or covariates. Designing reliable measurement instruments, using multiple data sources, and ensuring consistency in definitions are key to reducing this bias. Attrition bias particularly affects longitudinal observational studies where subjects drop out over time. If dropout is related to both treatment and outcome, causal inference is threatened. Planning strategies such as follow up protocols, incentives for continued participation, and methods for handling missing data must therefore be part of study design. Another vital strategy is transparency and pre-registration. By articulating hypotheses, analytic plans, and confounder selection strategies before examining outcomes, researchers reduce risks of data driven choices that inflate bias. Pre-registration does not eliminate confounding but strengthens credibility by committing to design choices in advance. Altogether these strategies form a toolkit that transforms observational studies from mere data description into structured approximations of causal inference. Reducing confounding and bias is not a single step but a layered set of design considerations that interact. Proper planning in this stage establishes a foundation upon which analytic methods can operate with integrity. Without such planning statistical techniques become superficial adjustments for deeper flaws.

Observational studies thrive when design anticipates and neutralizes confounding and bias to the greatest extent possible.

Building Robust Cohorts and Sampling Strategies

The creation of cohorts in observational studies is a decisive act because it defines the population through which causal questions are investigated. A cohort is essentially a group of individuals who share a common characteristic or experience during a defined period of time. In the context of causal inference, building robust cohorts ensures that treatment and comparison groups are clearly defined, temporally ordered, and sufficiently representative. A strong cohort design begins with explicit definition of eligibility criteria. These criteria establish who enters the study and who does not and therefore shape both internal and external validity. Eligibility must be guided by the causal question, ensuring that subjects have the potential to experience both the treatment and the outcome. Overly broad criteria risk heterogeneity that complicates inference, while overly narrow criteria may limit generalizability. Balance between inclusivity and precision is necessary. Sampling strategies determine how individuals are selected into cohorts. Random sampling is ideal for representativeness but often impractical in real world data contexts where records are preexisting. Stratified sampling allows for representation across key subgroups, ensuring sufficient sample sizes for subgroup analysis. Cluster sampling may be necessary when units are naturally grouped such as schools, hospitals, or neighborhoods. Each approach must be aligned with the causal objective and the constraints of available data. Another crucial design decision is how to define treatment and comparison groups. In observational studies treatment is not assigned but observed, so clarity is needed about what constitutes exposure. Ambiguity in definitions weakens inference because subjects may be misclassified. Cohorts must therefore establish clear operational criteria for exposure status and ensure that they can be measured reliably. Equally important is ensuring that exposure precedes outcome measurement to maintain causal directionality. Cohort building also requires strategies to address time varying exposures and outcomes. Unlike cross sectional designs, many causal questions unfold dynamically over time. For example, the effect of a policy intervention on economic outcomes may vary with duration of exposure or may change across historical periods. Time varying designs require longitudinal cohorts that capture repeated measurements and align exposure windows with outcome assessments. Sampling strategies for such designs must anticipate attrition and implement protocols to maintain engagement over time. Representativeness is another dimension. If cohorts are drawn from narrow contexts such as specific hospitals or geographic regions, findings may not generalize. Researchers must decide whether the goal is internal validity for a specific population or broader external validity. When generalizability is desired, sampling must extend across diverse contexts, adjusting for structural factors that shape treatment assignment. Cohort robustness also depends on sample size. Too small a sample undermines statistical power while excessively large samples may create false precision without addressing bias. Power calculations and feasibility assessments should therefore guide cohort size. Another layer involves data quality. Cohorts built from electronic records or administrative databases may suffer from missing values, coding errors, or inconsistent definitions. Robust design requires validation studies, cross checking with alternative data sources, and clear documentation of measurement processes. Cohorts must also account for clustering and dependencies in data. Individuals within families, communities, or institutions are not independent and failure to account for these structures introduces bias. Multilevel designs or sampling strategies that recognize clustering provide more accurate causal inference. Ethical considerations again play a role. Informed consent, protection of privacy, and responsible use of sensitive information are indispensable when building cohorts. The rights of participants must remain central even when data appears to be readily available from institutional records. Transparent communication about study purpose and limitations also builds trust in the research process. Ultimately the robustness of causal inference in observational studies rests on the soundness of cohort construction and sampling. These are not trivial technical details but core determinants of credibility. A poorly defined cohort produces biased estimates regardless of analytical sophistication. A well designed cohort aligned with thoughtful sampling strategies provides the fertile ground upon which causal analysis grows. In causal inference the design of cohorts and samples is not simply preliminary work but the very structure that determines the strength of every subsequent conclusion.

Chapter Three

Counterfactual Reasoning and the Potential Outcomes Framework

At the heart of causal inference lies counterfactual reasoning which attempts to answer the fundamental question of what would have happened to an individual or unit under a different treatment condition. Since one cannot observe both treated and untreated states for the same individual simultaneously, causal inference constructs a conceptual framework of potential outcomes. For each unit there exists a potential outcome under treatment and a potential outcome under control. The causal effect is defined as the difference between these two potential outcomes. The challenge is that only one of these potential outcomes is ever observed in reality while the other remains a counterfactual. This is known as the fundamental problem of causal inference. To overcome this, researchers rely on assumptions and study designs that allow them to approximate what the unobserved counterfactual would have been. The potential outcomes framework also known as the Rubin Causal Model provides a rigorous language for articulating these assumptions. It formalizes causal inference as a problem of missing data and frames the goal as estimating the average treatment effect across a population or subpopulation. By defining causal effects in terms of potential outcomes the framework separates causal questions from specific statistical models, making it broadly applicable across disciplines. The key assumptions underpinning this framework are crucial to understand. One central assumption is consistency which states that the observed outcome for a unit under the treatment actually received equals the potential outcome under that treatment. This assumption sounds trivial but ensures that treatments are well defined and that variations in implementation are not conflated with different treatments. Another critical assumption is ignobility or confoundedness which posits that given a set of observed covariates treatment assignment is independent of potential outcomes. This means that once relevant covariates are controlled for, treatment and control groups are comparable. Ignitability cannot be tested directly and therefore relies on substantive domain knowledge and careful study design. The assumption of positivity or overlap is equally important. It requires that for every combination of covariates there exists a non-zero probability of receiving each treatment condition. Without overlap it becomes impossible to make comparisons because certain types of individuals never appear in both treatment and control groups. Violations of positivity manifest as extrapolation where estimates rely on unobserved counterfactuals. Within this framework causal inference is achieved by estimating the missing potential outcomes through comparison of similar units across treatment conditions. Techniques such as matching, weighting, stratification, and regression adjustment emerge as methods for constructing approximations of these counterfactuals. Each method aims to restore comparability by balancing covariates so that observed outcomes in the control group can serve as proxies for unobserved outcomes in the treatment group and vice versa. The potential outcomes framework also clarifies the distinction between average treatment effects and conditional treatment effects. The average treatment effect is the mean difference in potential outcomes across the entire population. Conditional treatment effects focus on subgroups defined by covariates. These distinctions matter because causal effects are rarely homogeneous. In practice the framework emphasizes explicitness. Researchers must clearly state which potential outcomes are being estimated, under which assumptions, and for which population. This explicitness avoids the common trap of interpreting associations as causal without grounding them in counterfactual reasoning. The counterfactual perspective also provides a foundation for understanding bias. Selection bias occurs when treated and control groups differ systematically in ways related to outcomes, making observed outcomes poor proxies for counterfactuals. Confounding bias arises when variables influence both treatment assignment and outcomes, violating ignobility. Measurement error creates discrepancies between observed and true covariates, undermining assumptions of balance. Recognizing these biases through the potential outcomes lens enables systematic strategies to address them. Importantly the potential outcomes framework extends beyond binary treatments. It generalizes to multi valued treatments, continuous treatments, and even dynamic treatment regimens where treatment may evolve over time. This flexibility makes it applicable across diverse domains from medicine to economics to social science. By situating causal inference within the structured logic of counterfactuals the potential outcomes framework transforms vague causal claims into precise sentiments. It highlights the central challenge that we cannot observe both potential outcomes for the same unit but through careful design, assumptions, and analysis we can approximate them with rigor. Counterfactual reasoning does not eliminate uncertainty but provides the conceptual clarity necessary to pursue causality in observational data with intellectual honesty and methodological precision.

Graphical Models and Causal Diagrams

Graphical models particularly directed acyclic graphs have revolutionized the practice of causal inference by offering a visual and mathematical representation of relationships among variables. Unlike traditional statistical models that rely heavily on algebraic notation, causal diagrams provide intuitive clarity about the structure of causal systems. Each node in a directed acyclic graph represents a variable and each directed edge represents a causal influence. The absence of cycles ensures that the graph reflects a coherent temporal or logical ordering. Causal diagrams serve multiple purposes in observational studies. First they provide a framework for identifying confounders. By tracing back door paths between treatment and outcome, researchers can see which variables need to be controlled to block spurious associations. The back door criterion formalizes this principle by stating that a set of variables blocks all back door paths if and only if conditioning on them renders treatment independent of unobserved potential outcomes. This principle allows researchers to decide systematically which covariates to include in their analysis rather than relying on arbitrary or purely statistical criteria. Graphical models also clarify the dangers of adjusting for inappropriate variables. Controlling for colliders, variables that are influenced by both treatment and outcome, can introduce bias rather than eliminate it. Similarly controlling for mediators that lie on the causal pathway can distort estimates of total causal effects. Causal diagrams therefore serve as a safeguard against misguided adjustment strategies by distinguishing confounders from colliders and mediators. Another important contribution of causal diagrams is their ability to guide identification of instruments. By inspecting the graph one can see whether a candidate variable influences treatment but not the outcome except through treatment, satisfying the conditions for a valid instrumental variable. Graphical tools thus support creative strategies for addressing unmeasured confounding. Beyond identification, causal diagrams integrate with formal rules of do calculus which allow researchers to derive causal effects from observational data under specific assumptions. Do calculus provides a set of rules for manipulating probability distributions in the presence of interventions, essentially bridging graphical intuition with algebraic rigor. This connection elevates causal diagrams from informal sketches to formal scientific tools. Graphical models also highlight the limits of inference. They reveal when causal effects are not identifiable given the available data and assumptions. This transparency prevents overconfident claims and directs research toward feasible questions. In observational settings where randomization is absent, such clarity is invaluable. Graphical thinking also enhances communication. Complex causal relationships that may be opaque in text or equations become more accessible when visualized. Diagrams facilitate dialogue among researchers, policymakers, and practitioners, ensuring that assumptions about causal structure are explicit and open to critique. Importantly causal diagrams do not replace domain knowledge. They are only as valid as the causal structures they represent. Constructing an accurate graph requires substantive expertise about the processes generating the data. Inaccurate diagrams lead to misleading conclusions. Yet by forcing researchers to articulate assumptions explicitly they improve scientific transparency. The integration of graphical models into causal inference also expands to advanced contexts. For instance dynamic treatment regimens with time varying exposures can be represented with extended graphs that capture sequential decision processes. Latent variable models can be embedded to represent unobserved confounders. Graphical causal models also underpin modern algorithms in machine learning that aim to recover causal structures from high dimensional data, linking traditional causal inference with contemporary computational methods. In observational research where confounding and selection bias are pervasive, causal diagrams provide a compass. They allow researchers to navigate the maze of potential relationships, clarify which paths represent causal influence, and determine which must be blocked to reveal the true effect. They also bridge theory with empirical strategies by guiding variable selection and model specification. Without graphical clarity, attempts to infer causality from observational data risk becoming arbitrary adjustments that fail to capture the underlying structure. With causal diagrams, inference gains a principled foundation that integrates intuition, mathematics, and transparency.

Structural Models and Identification Strategies

Structural models form another pillar of analytical frameworks for causal inference by explicitly encoding causal mechanisms into mathematical relationships. Unlike purely statistical models that aim to capture correlations, structural models seek to represent the underlying data generating process. They formalize assumptions about how variables influence one another and in doing so they provide a route to causal identification in observational data. Structural equation models are a common form where each variable is expressed as a function of its causes plus an error term. These models can be specified in either linear or nonlinear forms and can include both observed and latent variables. By combining structural assumptions with observed data, researchers can estimate causal parameters that correspond to theoretical mechanisms. Identification is the central challenge in structural modeling. A model is identified if the causal parameters can be uniquely determined from the joint distribution of observed variables given the assumed structure. Identification requires that the system of equations is not underdetermined and that the causal paths are distinguishable. Techniques such as instrumental variables, exclusion restrictions, and rank conditions are employed to achieve identification. Instrumental variable strategies are particularly important in observational studies where unmeasured confounding is a persistent problem. An instrument is a variable that influences treatment but has no direct effect on the outcome except through treatment. When valid instruments exist they provide a way to mimic randomization and identify causal effects even in the presence of unmeasured confounders. However the validity of instruments is a strong assumption and often difficult to verify empirically. Exclusion restrictions within structural models specify that certain variables influence only subsets of the system. These restrictions reduce complexity and aid identification by narrowing down possible parameter values. Functional form assumptions, such as linearity, are also sometimes invoked though they carry risks if the true relationships are nonlinear. Structural models extend beyond simple cause effect relationships to represent feedback loops, mediation, and moderation. For example in economics structural models represent supply and demand systems where price and quantity influence each other simultaneously. In social sciences they capture pathways through which education influences earnings both directly and indirectly via skill acquisition. Such models provide deeper insights into mechanisms rather than mere average treatment effects. The interplay between structural models and causal diagrams is also noteworthy. Graphical models specify qualitative relationships while structural models quantify them. Together they provide a complete toolkit for reasoning about causality. Structural models can be visualized through diagrams, and diagrams can be translated into equations, reinforcing coherence across methodologies. Modern advances extend structural modeling into high dimensional and computational settings. Bayesian structural models incorporate prior knowledge and uncertainty. Machine learning methods can be integrated to estimate complex functional forms while retaining causal interpretability. These innovations expand the reach of structural inference to large scale observational datasets. Nevertheless structural modeling is not free from limitations. Results hinge critically on the validity of assumptions. Misspecification of equations or invalid instruments can produce misleading conclusions. Transparency about assumptions, sensitivity analysis, and robustness checks are therefore essential. Despite these challenges structural models provide a powerful lens for causal inference in observational studies. They transform correlations into mechanistic explanations, allow estimation of parameters that align with theory, and provide strategies for overcoming confounding. In domains where policy decisions, medical interventions, or economic reforms depend on understanding not just whether but how variables influence one another, structural models deliver indispensable insights. Identification strategies embedded within these models ensure that causal claims rest on solid ground rather than speculative associations. Observational data itself cannot yield causality but when combined with structural assumptions, instruments, and restrictions it becomes a source of rigorous causal knowledge. The analytical frameworks of counterfactual reasoning, causal diagrams, and structural modeling together constitute a comprehensive foundation for causal inference. Each brings unique strengths: potential outcomes provide conceptual clarity, diagrams guide identification and adjustment, and structural models formalize mechanisms. Their integration allows observational studies to move beyond descriptive analysis into the rigorous domain of causal discovery.

Chapter Four

Understanding the Nature of Hidden Confounders

Hidden confounders are among the most persistent challenges in causal inference because they represent variables that influence both the treatment and the outcome but remain unobserved or unmeasured within the data. Their presence introduces bias that can easily distort estimates of causal effects, making relationships appear stronger or weaker than they truly are, or even reversing their direction. To understand the complexity of hidden confounders one must first recognize the fundamental difficulty they impose on observational research. Unlike randomized experiments where randomization theoretically balances both observed and unobserved variables across treatment groups, observational studies lack this luxury. As a result, unobserved variables that correlate with both the independent and dependent variables can lead to spurious associations. A classic example is the relationship between ice cream sales and drowning deaths. Observationally one might conclude that ice cream consumption causes drowning, yet the hidden confounder here is temperature. Hot weather increases both ice cream consumption and swimming activity which in turn raises the risk of drowning. If temperature is not observed and accounted for, the analyst might wrongly attribute drowning risk to ice cream consumption. This illustrates how misleading results can be without careful attention to hidden confounding. To deepen the appreciation of the problem one must explore the structural role of confounders in causal diagrams. Directed acyclic graphs, or DAGs, represent variables as nodes and causal relations as arrows. In such graphs a confounder is a variable with arrows pointing to both the treatment and the outcome. If that confounder is unmeasured the backdoor path it creates cannot be blocked, meaning that associations along that path contaminate the estimate of causal effects. The difficulty arises because one cannot simply include what is unmeasured in the model. In practice researchers often rely on proxies, sensitivity analysis, or instrumental variable techniques to mitigate the effects of hidden confounding. However none of these strategies fully eliminate the inherent uncertainty caused by what remains unobserved. In addition the severity of confounding bias depends on the strength of the associations the hidden variable has with both the treatment and the outcome. When these correlations are strong the distortion is severe, when they are weak the distortion may be negligible. But without measurement one cannot know the magnitude with confidence, leaving the door open for skepticism about any causal claims made from purely observational data. In health research hidden confounders are particularly troublesome. Consider the study of a new drug's effectiveness in real-world settings. Patients who receive the drug might systematically differ from those who do not in terms of socioeconomic status, access to care, or underlying health behaviors. Many of these variables may not be fully captured in administrative data. For instance lifestyle variables like exercise frequency or stress levels may be omitted but still influence both treatment assignment and health outcomes. This creates the possibility of overstating or understating the drug's impact. Similarly in social sciences hidden confounders can stem from unmeasured psychological or cultural factors. When evaluating the effect of education on earnings for example unobserved ability, motivation, or family support may simultaneously influence both years of schooling and future income. Failing to account for them risks attributing wage differences to education alone when part of the difference may arise from these latent factors. The challenge extends to economics where policy interventions such as tax cuts, subsidies, or welfare reforms are often studied using nonexperimental data. Hidden confounders such as political preferences, informal networks, or local enforcement practices can confound relationships, leading analysts to overestimate or underestimate policy effectiveness. In machine learning and artificial intelligence applications where massive observational datasets are processed hidden confounders represent perhaps the most subtle yet dangerous source of bias. Automated algorithms may identify patterns and correlations but without causal reasoning these patterns might merely reflect the influence of unobserved variables. For example predictive policing algorithms might suggest higher crime risk in certain neighborhoods based on observed arrests, but hidden confounders such as differential policing intensity across regions may actually drive the observed correlations. If unacknowledged this could lead to reinforcement of biases rather than genuine causal understanding. Philosophically the existence of hidden confounders forces a reflection on the limits of human knowledge and the epistemic boundaries of inference from incomplete data. The fundamental problem of causal inference reminds us that we can only observe one potential outcome for each unit under one treatment condition. The missing counterfactual combined with the possibility of unobserved influences means that absolute certainty is unattainable. The best we can do is approximate causal truth within the limits of our assumptions and methodological tools. Thus, any researcher engaging with observational data must cultivate humility about conclusions drawn, and transparency in acknowledging where hidden confounding might compromise validity. Hidden confounders also raise questions about research ethics. Overconfident claims in the presence of unobserved bias can mislead policymakers, clinicians, or business leaders into making poor decisions with real consequences. For example overstating the benefits of a health intervention without addressing possible hidden confounding could encourage widespread adoption of an ineffective treatment, wasting resources and endangering lives. Similarly in public policy adopting reforms based on biased evidence could create social harm rather than progress. Therefore honesty about uncertainty and caution in interpretation is not just an academic exercise but a moral responsibility. Understanding hidden confounders also requires examining historical cases where failure to account for them led to false conclusions. For example early epidemiological studies once suggested that hormone replacement therapy reduced cardiovascular risk among postmenopausal women. However subsequent randomized controlled trials revealed that the apparent benefit was largely due to hidden confounding by socioeconomic status and health-seeking behavior. Women choosing hormone therapy were wealthier and more health conscious than those who did not, leading to confounded observational results. Another famous case involves smoking and lung cancer research. For years skeptics argued that the correlation between smoking and cancer could be explained by a genetic predisposition that caused both smoking behavior and cancer risk. Though eventually evidence overwhelmingly supported the causal role of smoking, the debate highlighted how hidden confounding can cloud causal claims. The challenge of hidden confounders therefore remains central to the philosophy and practice of causal inference. Without recognition of their role and strategies to address them, observational research risks becoming a source of misleading correlations rather than genuine causal insights. Acknowledging them, modeling them explicitly when possible, and quantifying their potential impact when not directly observable are essential steps toward strengthening the credibility of causal analysis in the wild.

Strategies for Detecting and Mitigating Hidden Confounders

Once the reality of hidden confounders is recognized the next question becomes how to detect their presence and mitigate their effects. Though truly unobserved confounders cannot be measured directly researchers have developed a variety of strategies to approximate their influence. One powerful approach involves instrumental variables. An instrumental variable is one that affects the treatment but has no direct effect on the outcome except through that treatment. By leveraging such variables one can isolate variation in the treatment that is independent of confounders. For example in studying the effect of education on income distance to the nearest college can sometimes serve as an instrument. Living closer increases the likelihood of attending college but distance itself has little direct effect on later wages aside from its influence on educational attainment. This method, however, depends heavily on the validity of the instrument. If the instrument also affects the outcome through other channels it fails, reintroducing bias. Another strategy involves natural experiments where external shocks or random-like events create quasi-random treatment assignment. Examples include lottery admissions to schools, draft lotteries for military service, or sudden policy changes applied to some regions but not others. These designs mimic randomization and reduce the influence of hidden confounders though they require careful justification that the event indeed approximates randomness. Sensitivity analysis provides yet another approach. Instead of eliminating confounding it quantifies how strong an unobserved confounder would have to be to explain away the observed association. This does not solve the problem but allows researchers to gauge the robustness of their findings. If only an implausibly strong confounder could account for the observed effect the evidence for causality strengthens. Conversely if a weak confounder could overturn the result the claim must be treated with caution. Propensity score methods, although primarily designed for observed confounders can indirectly reveal issues with hidden ones. When balancing observed covariates still leaves residual imbalance in outcomes, it raises suspicion that unobserved factors may also be at play. Researchers can use balance diagnostics and placebo tests to explore whether hidden bias might exist. For example one might test whether the treatment predicts outcomes that it should not plausibly affect. If it does, hidden confounding is likely present.

Another mitigation strategy is the use of longitudinal data and fixed effects models. By following the same units over time and accounting for time-invariant unobserved characteristics, researchers can reduce confounding. For example when studying the effect of job training on wages unobserved ability may bias cross-sectional comparisons. However within-person comparisons across time help to control stable individual traits, limiting confounding from those sources. Similarly difference in differences designs exploit before-and-after comparisons across treated and untreated groups. If parallel trends assumptions hold this method can reduce bias from hidden confounders that remain constant over time. Machine learning methods are increasingly being applied to detect signals of hidden confounding. Latent variable models attempt to infer the presence of unmeasured factors from patterns in observed data. While promising these methods still depend on assumptions and cannot replace direct measurement. They may, however, complement traditional approaches by highlighting suspicious correlations that might reflect unobserved influences. Triangulation across multiple study designs also helps mitigate the threat of hidden confounders. When different methodological approaches converge on similar conclusions confidence increases that the results are not entirely driven by unobserved bias. For instance if both an instrumental variable analysis and a difference in differences approach suggest the same direction and magnitude of effect, the causal claim gains credibility. Another practical strategy involves careful data collection. While the term hidden confounder implies something unobserved, in reality many so-called hidden variables remain unmeasured simply because of inadequate study design. Investing in richer data that captures behavioral, social, psychological, and contextual factors can reduce the number of hidden variables. For example in health research adding lifestyle surveys to clinical data improves adjustment for potential confounders like diet, exercise, and stress. In economics including measures of informal networks and local institutions strengthens causal inference. In social science incorporating cultural and attitudinal surveys helps capture otherwise hidden influences. The researcher's theoretical framework also plays a key role. Causal diagrams guide the identification of potential confounders before analysis begins. By systematically mapping out possible variables that influence both treatment and outcome one can design strategies to measure and adjust for them. The failure to theorize about hidden confounders often results in flawed conclusions not because the confounders are unknowable but because they were not anticipated. Ethical responsibility also dictates that analysts must communicate the limits of their strategies for dealing with hidden confounders. Claiming certainty where only sensitivity has been performed is misleading. Researchers should openly report assumptions, robustness checks, and alternative explanations. Policymakers and practitioners who rely on such evidence must be made aware of the potential for residual confounding, so that decisions are made with full understanding of uncertainty. The combination of statistical ingenuity, careful data design, theoretical clarity, and ethical transparency forms the best defense against hidden confounders. While no strategy can eliminate them entirely the cumulative weight of these approaches can substantially reduce their impact. They remind us that causal inference in observational studies is as much about disciplined humility and methodological rigor as it is about technical sophistication. Each tool, whether instrumental variables, natural experiments, or sensitivity analysis, represents a way to chip away at the fog created by hidden confounders. None delivers perfect clarity but together they illuminate enough of the landscape to allow cautious yet meaningful navigation.

Implications of Hidden Confounders for Real-World Decision Making

The presence of hidden confounders does not merely complicate academic debates. It has profound implications for real-world decision making in health, economics, public policy, education, and technology. Decisions guided by observational evidence directly affect lives and resources. If hidden confounders distort findings the consequences can be severe. In medicine reliance on observational studies with unmeasured confounding risks exposing patients to ineffective or harmful treatments. For instance if a drug appears beneficial in observational data but the effect is confounded by patient characteristics adoption at scale can lead to wasted expenditures and false hope. The hormone replacement therapy case illustrates this vividly. Similarly in assessing the risks of new exposures such as environmental pollutants hidden confounding can either exaggerate or mask true harms. Policymakers relying on such data may underregulate harmful substances or overregulate benign ones, with both health and economic costs. In economics decisions about taxation, welfare, and labor markets often hinge on evidence derived from observational data. Hidden confounders in such analyses can misguide policy. For example a study might suggest that lowering taxes increases investment but hidden confounders like global economic cycles could actually drive the observed correlation. If policymakers mistakenly attribute the boom to tax policy they may entrench ineffective strategies while ignoring structural causes. In education hidden confounders complicate evaluations of programs intended to improve student outcomes. Charter school effectiveness studies often confront confounding from parental motivation or community support. If not addressed these biases can lead policymakers to overstate the benefits of certain educational models, directing resources away from equally or more effective alternatives. In technology the stakes of hidden confounders manifest in algorithmic decision making. Predictive systems trained on biased observational data inherit confounding problems. Credit scoring algorithms may link loan repayment with demographic proxies rather than true financial reliability. Hiring algorithms may confuse educational pedigree with productivity due to unobserved social capital. Without deliberate correction these systems propagate hidden confounder bias at scale, reinforcing inequalities under the guise of objectivity. Businesses also face risks. A company that misattributes sales increases to a marketing campaign when in fact they are driven by unobserved seasonal demand may waste millions scaling ineffective strategies. Similarly online platforms that attribute user retention to design tweaks while ignoring hidden confounders such as broader cultural trends may misallocate engineering resources. The implications extend to ethics and social trust. When institutions make decisions based on flawed causal inferences the public may lose confidence in science, government, and industry. For example when conflicting health advice emerges due to hidden confounders people may become skeptical of all expert guidance, fueling misinformation. Recognizing the role of hidden confounders and communicating uncertainty transparently can help preserve trust. For decision makers the lesson is not to abandon observational evidence but to treat it with caution. Incorporating robustness checks, triangulating across methods, and investing in richer data can strengthen confidence. Decision makers must also be trained to interpret findings probabilistically rather than as definitive truths. For example instead of proclaiming a policy will certainly improve employment, policymakers can frame the evidence as suggestive but subject to potential unobserved biases. Such humility not only reflects reality more accurately but also conditions the public to understand science as a process rather than a series of final verdicts. The presence of hidden confounders also underscores the value of continued investment in randomized controlled trials where feasible. While expensive and sometimes impractical they remain the most reliable method for eliminating unobserved confounding. Observational evidence can guide hypotheses and identify patterns but should ideally be complemented by experimental confirmation whenever possible. Finally the challenge of hidden confounders highlights the importance of interdisciplinary collaboration. Statisticians, data scientists, domain experts, and philosophers of science must work together to anticipate, detect, and adjust for hidden biases. Each brings a unique perspective, from technical methods to theoretical frameworks to ethical considerations. Only through such collaboration can the full complexity of hidden confounding be addressed in a way that makes observational causal inference both credible and useful. Thus the implications of hidden confounders stretch far beyond academic theory. They touch upon the lives of patients, the stability of economies, the fairness of education, the accountability of governments, and the integrity of technologies. Confronting them with seriousness, humility, and methodological rigor is therefore not optional but essential for any researcher or practitioner committed to using observational data to inform decisions.

Chapter Five

The Logic and Power of Instrumental Variables

Instrumental variables represent one of the most powerful strategies in causal inference for addressing unobserved confounding. The intuition behind them is both elegant and demanding. Suppose we wish to estimate the causal effect of a treatment on an outcome but are concerned that hidden confounders bias the relationship. An instrumental variable provides a source of variation in the treatment that is independent of these confounders, allowing us to isolate the causal effect. The instrument must satisfy two critical conditions. First it must be strongly correlated with the treatment, known as the relevance condition. Without relevance the instrument cannot generate meaningful variation in the treatment and thus fails to provide identification. Second it must affect the outcome only through the treatment and not through any other channel, known as the exclusion restriction. This is the more challenging requirement because it is difficult to prove conclusively. A valid instrument allows us to mimic the logic of randomization in an otherwise observational setting by leveraging variation in the treatment that is as good as random with respect to unobserved confounders. Consider the classic example of education and earnings. Education levels are not randomly assigned. Individuals who pursue more schooling may differ systematically in ability, motivation, or family support, all of which also affect income. These unobserved factors confound the relationship. Distance to the nearest college has often been used as an instrument. Living closer increases the likelihood of attending college but plausibly has little direct impact on future income except through educational attainment. By using variation in distance researchers can isolate the part of education not influenced by unobserved traits, thus estimating its causal effect on earnings. Another famous case is the draft lottery in the United States during the Vietnam War. Birth dates randomly determined draft eligibility. This exogenous variation influenced the probability of military service but should not otherwise affect long-term outcomes such as earnings or health. Thus draft lottery numbers served as an instrument for military service, enabling causal analysis of its consequences. Instrumental variables are not limited to social sciences. In medicine genetic variants have been used as instruments in Mendelian randomization studies. Because genetic variants are randomly assigned at conception they can provide natural experiments for estimating causal effects of risk factors on health outcomes. For example certain genetic variants influence cholesterol levels. By using them as instruments researchers can estimate the causal effect of cholesterol on heart disease while avoiding confounding from lifestyle factors. In economics rainfall variation has been employed as an instrument for agricultural income, enabling causal studies of the relationship between income shocks and social outcomes such as education or fertility. These examples reveal the breadth of instrumental variable applications across domains. Yet despite their appeal the method has significant limitations. Weak instruments pose a major problem. If the instrument is only weakly correlated with the treatment estimates become biased and imprecise. This is especially problematic when multiple instruments are used, as weak instruments can collectively magnify bias. Furthermore the exclusion restriction is often more an assumption than a verifiable fact. For instance does living near a college truly affect income only through education? Proximity might also influence job networks, urban exposure, or cultural capital, violating the exclusion restriction. Similarly draft eligibility might influence long-term outcomes not only through military service but also through psychological stress or political engagement. Assessing validity requires careful theoretical reasoning, robustness checks, and often convincing narratives more than empirical proof. Another subtle challenge lies in interpreting instrumental variable estimates. Because instruments identify causal effects for the subpopulation whose treatment is influenced by the instrument, the resulting estimate is a local average treatment effect or LATE. For instance using college proximity as an instrument identifies the effect of education for those individuals whose decision to attend college depends on distance. This may not generalize to all individuals. Similarly draft lotteries identify the effect of military service on those induced into service by the lottery, not necessarily on volunteers. Thus instrumental variables provide valid causal inference but often with limited external validity. Researchers and policymakers must recognize this distinction. The method is therefore not a universal solution but a powerful complement to other approaches. Its strength lies in transforming naturally occurring or designed variation into quasi-experiments that circumvent hidden confounding. But it requires creativity in identifying valid instruments, discipline in defending assumptions, and humility in interpreting results. When these conditions are met instrumental variables illuminate causal relationships that would otherwise remain obscured.

The Role of Natural Experiments in Causal Inference

Natural experiments extend the same logic as instrumental variables but in broader form. They exploit events, policies, or shocks that approximate random assignment of treatments to units. These events are not designed by researchers but occur in the real world, providing opportunities to study causal effects in observational data. The defining feature of a natural experiment is that assignment to treatment is plausibly exogenous, meaning independent of confounders, at least within certain subgroups or contexts. One classic natural experiment arises from policy changes that affect some regions or groups but not others. For example the introduction of minimum wage laws in certain states provides a natural experiment for studying employment effects by comparing outcomes before and after the policy in treated versus untreated states. Card and Krueger's influential study of fast food restaurants in New Jersey and Pennsylvania is a famous example. Similarly the expansion of Medicaid in some states but not others offers opportunities to assess the impact of health insurance on access to care and health outcomes. Natural disasters also function as natural experiments. Earthquakes, hurricanes, or floods strike certain areas but not others, often with some degree of randomness. By comparing affected and unaffected populations researchers can study the causal impact of shocks on economic resilience, health, or migration. For instance Hurricane Katrina's devastation of New Orleans provided a natural experiment for examining the long-term effects of displacement on educational outcomes and labor markets. Historical events further illustrate the power of natural experiments. The fall of the Berlin Wall and German reunification created a sudden and exogenous change in economic and political institutions. This allowed researchers to study the causal effects of capitalism and democracy on formerly socialist populations. Similarly the partition of India and Pakistan created exogenous shifts in borders and populations, enabling analysis of the long-term consequences of displacement and forced migration. Natural experiments also arise from administrative rules. For example school entry cutoff dates create arbitrary thresholds determining whether children start school earlier or later depending on their birth month. These cutoffs serve as natural experiments for studying the causal effect of age at school entry on academic achievement or later life outcomes. Likewise tax policy changes that depend on income thresholds or geographic boundaries provide exogenous variation suitable for causal analysis. The strength of natural experiments lies in their ability to approximate randomization without the need for costly or impractical controlled trials. They leverage real-world variation in ways that reveal causal mechanisms otherwise hidden by confounding. Importantly they often address questions of major social or policy relevance since they arise from real events and institutional changes. However natural experiments are not without weaknesses. Exogeneity must be carefully defended. For instance when studying the impact of Medicaid expansion researchers must argue that expansion decisions were not correlated with unobserved factors affecting health outcomes. If states choosing expansion were systematically different from those that did not, the assumption of exogeneity is compromised. Similarly natural disasters may not be entirely random. Areas prone to hurricanes may also differ systematically in socioeconomic conditions or infrastructure, confounding the analysis. Another challenge lies in spillover effects. When one group or region experiences a shock the consequences may extend to neighboring groups or markets, contaminating comparisons. For example when studying minimum wage changes in one state workers or firms may cross borders, diluting the treatment contrast. Additionally natural experiments often produce results specific to the context of the event. The causal effects of school entry age in one country may not generalize to others with different educational systems. Thus while natural experiments provide strong internal validity they may face external validity limitations similar to instrumental variables. Despite these challenges natural experiments have reshaped entire fields of research. They have enabled economists, political scientists, sociologists, and health researchers to make credible causal claims about critical issues. Their appeal lies in their grounding in real-world events, which not only enhances their policy relevance but also engages broader audiences. Policymakers often find evidence from natural experiments more persuasive than purely statistical adjustments because the treatment variation is tangible and understandable. For the practice of causal inference natural experiments demonstrate the value of creativity, adaptability, and opportunism. Researchers cannot always design the perfect randomized trial, but they can remain attentive to the shocks, rules, and changes that occur naturally in society and exploit them rigorously. This requires a blend of theoretical insight to recognize potential exogeneity, methodological skill to model the effects correctly, and practical wisdom to interpret results responsibly. Ultimately natural experiments remind us that the world itself is full of randomization, albeit imperfect. By recognizing and harnessing this randomness we expand the scope of causal inference beyond the laboratory and into the wild complexity of human societies.

Practical Applications and Limitations of Instrumental Variables and Natural Experiments

The application of instrumental variables and natural experiments in real-world contexts reveals both their immense potential and their inherent limitations. These methods have allowed researchers to answer questions that would otherwise remain inaccessible, yet they must be applied with rigor and interpreted with care. Consider the case of labor economics where debates over the impact of immigration on native wages and employment have raged for decades. Direct comparisons are confounded by the fact that immigrants do not randomly choose destinations. They often settle in areas with growing economies, which themselves affect wages. To address these researchers have used instrumental variables such as historical settlement patterns to predict current immigrant flows. By leveraging exogenous variation in immigration they isolate causal impacts on labor markets. Similarly natural experiments have been employed to study sudden refugee influxes, such as the arrival of Cuban refugees in Miami during the Mariel boatlift. These approaches reveal that the impact of immigration is often more nuanced and less negative than feared. In health economics instrumental variables and natural experiments have been indispensable for studying the returns to medical interventions. Randomized controlled trials are expensive and sometimes ethically infeasible. Thus researchers rely on natural experiments such as sudden expansions in insurance coverage or policy changes in drug subsidies. For instance the introduction of Medicare in the United States provided a natural experiment for assessing the effects of health insurance on hospital use and mortality. These studies have demonstrated the life-saving potential of health insurance while also highlighting unintended consequences such as cost inflation. Instrumental variables in medicine often take the form of physician prescribing patterns. If some physicians are more likely to prescribe a drug than others, patient exposure can be instrumented by physician preference rather than patient characteristics, reducing confounding. This method has been applied to estimate drug effectiveness in real-world settings, though it depends heavily on the assumption that physician preference influences outcomes only through treatment. In education policy natural experiments have illuminated the consequences of reforms such as school voucher programs or changes in compulsory schooling laws. These reforms often apply to specific cohorts or regions, enabling before-and-after comparisons across treated and untreated groups. Instrumental variables such as birth date cutoffs for school entry have also revealed long-term impacts of educational attainment on health, income, and civic participation. These findings have shaped policy debates about the value of schooling and the design of educational systems. In political science natural experiments such as close elections have provided insights into the causal impact of political power. When elections are narrowly decided assignment of office can be considered nearly random, allowing researchers to study the effect of incumbency on policy outcomes or governance quality. Similarly redistricting reforms or court decisions that alter electoral rules provide exogenous shocks enabling causal analysis of representation and democracy. Yet while applications are rich limitations must be acknowledged. Instrumental variables require strong theoretical justification, and weak instruments undermine credibility. Natural experiments depend on context-specific exogeneity that may be contested. Both methods often produce estimates with limited generalizability. Furthermore practical implementation can be complex. Identifying suitable instruments or natural experiments requires creativity and detailed knowledge of the domain. Analysts must also contend with imperfect compliance, measurement error, and heterogeneous treatment effects. Ethical considerations also arise. Natural disasters as instruments may yield valuable causal insights but the suffering they represent should not be trivialized. Researchers must approach such studies with sensitivity and respect. Similarly policy experiments that benefit some groups while disadvantaging others raise questions of fairness. Transparency in acknowledging these dimensions is essential for responsible research. Despite these caveats instrumental variables and natural experiments remain central pillars of modern causal inference. They provide the means to transform observational data into credible evidence of causality, guiding policy, medicine, education, and economics. Their value lies not in perfection but in their ability to approximate randomization when true randomization is impossible. They expand the toolkit of researchers navigating the wild terrain of observational data, offering pathways through the fog of hidden confounding. The practical lesson is that researchers must remain vigilant, imaginative, and disciplined. Valid instruments and natural experiments do not present themselves easily, but with theoretical grounding and methodological skill they can be identified and harnessed. Their application requires humility about limitations, yet their contributions to knowledge are undeniable. They remind us that causality, while elusive, can be uncovered when careful reasoning meets the randomness inherent in human affairs.

Chapter Six

The Evolution of Methods in Causal Inference

Causal inference has evolved from being a purely theoretical subject rooted in philosophy and abstract mathematics to becoming a powerful applied field that influences decision making in science, economics, social policy, medicine, and technology. The evolution of methods in this area reflects the ongoing need to refine our tools for identifying cause and effect relationships in environments where randomized controlled trials are either impractical or impossible. From the earliest attempts to understand causation through logical reasoning and counterfactuals, scholars sought clarity in disentangling correlation from causation, but the limitations of observation often constrained them. The introduction of probability theory created a new framework that allowed scholars to describe uncertainty and quantify relationships, but probability itself remained descriptive rather than explanatory. It was not until statisticians and economists began developing formal tools such as regression models that an analytical path to causal inference was set. Regression provided a structured way to compare groups while controlling for confounding variables, yet early implementations were fragile, often misrepresenting relationships when hidden biases existed. As data expanded in volume and variety, reliance on regression alone was no longer sufficient, and this gave rise to methods such as instrumental variables, propensity score matching, and difference-in-differences approaches. These methods attempted to replicate the counterfactual logic that underlies causality by constructing credible comparisons between treated and untreated groups under observational settings. Each step in the methodological evolution was a response to a fundamental problem: how can we simulate the conditions of an experiment when we cannot manipulate reality itself. Instrumental variables, for instance, addressed endogeneity by relying on external sources of variation, while propensity score matching sought to balance groups on observable characteristics, thereby approximating the fairness of random assignment. Difference-in-differences emerged from economics and social sciences to exploit natural variations across time, treating policy changes or shocks as quasi-experiments that allowed researchers to estimate effects in a comparative framework. The field advanced significantly with the formalization of causal diagrams, particularly through Judea Pearl's work, which introduced directed acyclic graphs as a way to visually and mathematically represent assumptions about causal relationships. These diagrams enabled clearer reasoning about which variables should be controlled for and which adjustments could introduce bias. By moving beyond equations and allowing a structural representation of causal systems, diagrams revolutionized the practice of causal inference, granting researchers tools to articulate and test assumptions more transparently. Today, the evolution of methods is characterized by the integration of machine learning into causal analysis. Algorithms that once served purely predictive goals are now being adapted to uncover causal mechanisms by exploiting patterns in high-dimensional data. These advancements allow researchers to manage complexities that traditional econometric models could not handle. Yet with these gains come new challenges, especially concerning interpretability, transparency, and the risk of automated systems obscuring the reasoning behind causal conclusions. The evolution of methods demonstrates that causal inference is a living discipline, continuously shaped by new data realities and computational capabilities, and that it remains central to advancing credible evidence across diverse domains.

Applications Across Disciplines

The impact of causal inference extends far beyond the confines of theoretical statistics and econometrics. Its principles underpin critical decisions in medicine, where observational studies guide treatments when trials are unfeasible. For instance, understanding the causal impact of lifestyle factors on health outcomes depends on carefully disentangling confounding influences like socioeconomic status, genetics, and environmental exposures. The medical field has long relied on epidemiology to approximate causal relationships, but recent advances in methods such as Mendelian randomization have allowed researchers to use genetic variation as instruments for estimating causal effects. This has opened pathways for understanding how risk factors influence disease outcomes with a robustness that purely observational methods could not previously achieve. In public policy, causal inference provides the backbone of program evaluation, where governments seek to measure whether interventions such as educational reforms, welfare programs, or tax incentives achieve their intended goals. Without the ability to infer causation, policy risks becoming a matter of guesswork, with resources potentially misallocated and unintended consequences overlooked. By using difference-in-differences techniques, natural experiments, or synthetic control methods, researchers provide policymakers with evidence that reflects more than correlation, strengthening the basis for effective governance. In economics, causal inference is central to understanding labor markets, development, and macroeconomic policies. Researchers investigate whether minimum wage laws affect employment, whether trade liberalization increases national productivity, or whether education drives long-term income growth. Each of these inquiries depends not only on measuring associations but on uncovering genuine causal links that guide theory and practice alike. In technology, causal inference is rapidly becoming a cornerstone of innovation. Tech companies apply causal reasoning to evaluate product changes, optimize digital platforms, and understand consumer behavior in ways that go beyond surface-level analytics. A recommendation algorithm that predicts preferences is valuable, but a causal system that can determine whether exposure to content causes engagement is far more powerful. This shift has encouraged the rise of experimentation culture, where companies routinely conduct randomized trials but also complement them with causal inference tools when trials are impractical or ethically constrained. In the social sciences, causal inference addresses long-standing questions about inequality, education, and cultural change. By applying advanced methods, sociologists and political scientists can better identify the causal structures that perpetuate disparities or explain voting patterns, offering insights into phenomena that shape societies at their core. Environmental science, too, increasingly draws on causal inference to evaluate the effects of policies on climate change, pollution reduction, and conservation efforts, areas where experimental designs are not only impossible but often ethically unacceptable. The expansion of applications demonstrates that causal inference is not simply a statistical exercise but a universal framework for structured reasoning in complex and uncertain environments. Its value lies in providing clarity where data alone cannot speak, ensuring that findings reflect genuine cause and effect rather than misleading correlations. This cross-disciplinary relevance explains why causal inference continues to attract attention, as its contributions resonate across every field that seeks to understand the consequences of decisions, actions, or natural phenomena.

Challenges and Future Directions

Despite its successes, causal inference faces significant challenges that shape its current practice and future trajectory. One of the most persistent challenges is the reliance on assumptions that are often untestable in practice. Every causal conclusion depends on a set of assumptions about the data generating process, the absence of hidden confounders, or the validity of instruments. If these assumptions fail, even the most sophisticated methods can yield biased or misleading results. This reality highlights the necessity of humility and transparency in causal work, where researchers must openly articulate and defend their assumptions. Another challenge is the rise of complex, high-dimensional data in modern science. While machine learning offers tools for managing vast datasets, the integration of these methods into causal frameworks raises questions about interpretability. Predictive algorithms may capture patterns, but causal inference demands clarity about mechanisms. Without careful adaptation, there is a risk that automated methods will obscure rather than illuminate causal relationships. Ethical challenges also weigh heavily on the field. As causal inference informs policy, healthcare, and technology, decisions derived from causal analyses can carry profound consequences for individuals and communities. Issues such as fairness, accountability, and equity must therefore be embedded within causal practice, ensuring that causal claims do not perpetuate inequalities or harm vulnerable populations. The increasing use of causal inference in artificial intelligence further complicates these concerns, as algorithms that influence millions of users daily must be evaluated not just for accuracy but for their causal impact on human behavior and well-being. Another ongoing issue is accessibility. Advanced causal inference requires technical expertise that can alienate practitioners in applied domains who need these insights most urgently. Bridging the gap between methodological sophistication and practical usability remains an important frontier. Developing intuitive tools, user-friendly software, and educational resources can democratize access, empowering more researchers and decision-makers to incorporate causal reasoning into their work. Looking to the future, several directions stand out as pivotal. One is the integration of causal inference with real-time decision-making systems, allowing for dynamic adaptation of policies or treatments as new data emerge. Another is the development of methods that can handle unstructured data such as text, images, and social networks, expanding the scope of causal inference into previously underexplored domains. Advances in computational power and interdisciplinary collaboration are also expected to push boundaries, enabling analyses of unprecedented scale and complexity. At the same time, philosophical debates about the very nature of causation continue to influence methodological development. Questions about whether causation is a feature of reality or a construct of human reasoning remain relevant, shaping how researchers justify and interpret causal claims. The challenge ahead is not only technical but conceptual, requiring ongoing dialogue between philosophy, statistics, and applied science. The future of causal inference lies in its ability to balance rigor with accessibility, precision with ethical responsibility, and innovation with interpretability. It is a discipline in constant motion, shaped by both the expanding possibilities of data and the timeless human need to understand the forces that govern outcomes. By confronting these challenges and pursuing thoughtful directions, causal inference will continue to unlock insights that guide progress across every realm of human endeavor.

Chapter Seven

Philosophical Underpinnings of Causality

The study of causality has roots that stretch deep into philosophy, long before statistics and mathematics began to formalize the questions we now associate with causal inference. Philosophers wrestled with the meaning of causation, asking not just how to detect it but whether it is a fundamental aspect of reality or simply a construct of human thought. Aristotle distinguished between different kinds of causes, ranging from material causes to final causes, laying the groundwork for the idea that causal reasoning is multifaceted rather than singular. Centuries later, David Hume famously argued that causation cannot be directly observed. For him, what we see are sequences of events, and our minds impose the notion of causality based on repeated associations. This skeptical perspective raised profound doubts about whether cause and effect can ever be definitively known or whether it is merely inferred through habit. Immanuel Kant responded by treating causality as a necessary condition for human experience, an innate category of the mind that structures how we perceive the world. These philosophical perspectives illustrate the enduring tension between empiricism and rationalism in causal reasoning, a tension that persists in modern debates. The rise of science in the seventeenth century added another dimension, as thinkers like Francis Bacon and Isaac Newton sought laws of nature that described causal relationships through experimentation and mathematical formulation. In this context, causality became not only a philosophical question but also a scientific necessity. Scientific progress demanded explanations that went beyond description, requiring mechanisms that could be tested and applied to new circumstances. Yet even as natural science advanced, the philosophical question of what causation truly is remained unresolved. In the twentieth century, logical positivists attempted to ground science in observation alone, sidelining metaphysical concepts like causality. However, the practical needs of science reasserted causation as indispensable, especially as fields like epidemiology and economics required structured reasoning about interventions and outcomes. Modern causal inference can thus be seen as a continuation of these philosophical debates, embedding them within formal mathematical frameworks while still grappling with the same fundamental issues. For example, the counterfactual model of causality, which asks what would have happened had an action not occurred, echoes Hume's skepticism about direct observation while providing a structured way to formalize his insights. Similarly, causal diagrams reflect Kant's idea that causality is a way of structuring knowledge, making assumptions explicit in a form that guides empirical analysis. Understanding these philosophical underpinnings is essential because it grounds causal inference in a broader intellectual tradition. It reminds us that causal claims are never merely technical but also conceptual, dependent on assumptions about how the world works and how humans can know it. The ongoing dialogue between philosophy and empirical science enriches causal inference, ensuring that it is not reduced to a set of formulas but is instead recognized as a fundamental mode of reasoning.

The Role of Counterfactuals in Modern Analysis

Counterfactual reasoning has become one of the central pillars of modern causal inference, offering a structured way to articulate the logic of cause and effect. At its core, the counterfactual approach asks a simple but profound question: what would have happened to the same unit of analysis had it experienced a different treatment or exposure. This question captures the essence of causality because causation implies a difference between actual outcomes and those that would have occurred under alternate circumstances. For example, when evaluating whether a medical treatment cures disease, the true causal effect is not observed directly because we cannot see the same patient both treated and untreated at the same time. Instead, we rely on constructing the counterfactual outcome, an imagined but formally defined scenario of what would have occurred under different conditions. The challenge lies in estimating these unobservable outcomes in ways that are credible and rigorous. The potential outcomes framework developed by statisticians such as Jerzy Neyman and Donald Rubin provided the mathematical foundation for counterfactual reasoning. Within this framework, every unit has two potential outcomes: one under treatment and one under control. Only one is observed, while the other remains counterfactual. This asymmetry defines the problem of causal inference: we are forever missing data about the alternate reality. To address this, causal inference relies on assumptions and methods that approximate what the counterfactual would have been. Randomized controlled trials achieve this by ensuring that treatment and control groups are equivalent on average, meaning the observed outcome for one group can stand in for the counterfactual of the other. In observational settings, the challenge is more formidable because selection into treatment is not random. Methods such as matching, regression adjustment, and instrumental variables attempt to replicate the logic of randomization by balancing or isolating variation in ways that approximate counterfactual outcomes. The power of counterfactual reasoning is that it provides a consistent language across these methods, unifying diverse approaches under a single conceptual framework. Beyond its methodological utility, counterfactual reasoning also offers practical advantages. It aligns closely with human intuition, as people naturally think in counterfactual terms when reflecting on decisions and outcomes. When someone says if only I had done things differently, they are engaging in counterfactual reasoning, imagining an alternate reality to understand the causal impact of their choice. This natural affinity strengthens the explanatory power of causal inference, making it both analytically rigorous and intuitively accessible. Counterfactuals are also critical in domains such as law, ethics, and policy, where responsibility often hinges on what would have happened under different circumstances. In legal reasoning, for example, establishing liability requires counterfactual judgment about whether harm would have occurred absent the defendant's actions. In policy, evaluating interventions requires considering what would have happened without them. By providing a formal framework for these judgments, counterfactual reasoning extends causal inference beyond technical statistics into the realm of human decision-making and accountability. Despite their power, counterfactuals come with challenges. Because they are inherently unobservable, every attempt to estimate them depends on assumptions that can never be fully verified. This makes transparency about assumptions crucial, as well as sensitivity analysis to evaluate how robust results are to possible violations. Advances in machine learning and computational modeling are now being applied to improve counterfactual estimation, allowing for greater precision in high-dimensional settings, though these methods still depend on careful design to avoid misleading conclusions. The role of counterfactuals in modern analysis demonstrates how causal inference straddles the line between the seen and the unseen, offering tools to reason rigorously about the realities we can never directly observe.

Building Bridges Between Theory and Practice

One of the enduring challenges in causal inference is bridging the gap between theoretical development and practical application. The theory of causal inference is rich, rigorous, and mathematically sophisticated, but the problems that practitioners face in fields like healthcare, policy, and business often involve messy data, imperfect measurements, and constraints that make ideal methods difficult to apply. The task, therefore, is not simply to advance theory but to translate it into practical tools that can inform real-world decisions. This bridge begins with clear communication. Theoretical advances such as directed acyclic graphs or the potential outcomes framework only achieve impact when practitioners can understand and apply them. This requires educational efforts, intuitive visualizations, and user-friendly software that reduce the cognitive barrier to entry. By lowering these barriers, causal inference becomes accessible not only to statisticians but also to doctors, policymakers, and business leaders who must make causal judgments in their work. Bridging theory and practice also involves adapting methods to the constraints of real data. For example, while ideal assumptions often include no hidden confounding, in practice hidden variables are almost always present. Researchers must therefore develop strategies for sensitivity analysis, robustness checks, and triangulation across multiple methods to strengthen confidence in conclusions. These adaptations are not deviations from theory but extensions of it, embodying the principle that rigorous reasoning must also be flexible. Case studies serve as another powerful bridge. By demonstrating how abstract methods can solve concrete problems, case studies illustrate the practical value of causal inference while also revealing the limitations of methods when applied in context. They create a feedback loop in which practical challenges inspire theoretical innovation, and theoretical tools, in turn, expand the capacity of practitioners. The rise of open science and interdisciplinary collaboration further strengthens this bridge. Causal inference thrives when statisticians, computer scientists, economists, and domain experts work together, combining methodological expertise with substantive knowledge. Interdisciplinary teams ensure that methods are not only technically sound but also contextually appropriate, grounded in the realities of the field to which they are applied. Finally, bridging theory and practice requires a cultural shift. In many applied fields, decision-making has long relied on descriptive statistics, correlations, and predictions. Encouraging a culture of causal reasoning means fostering awareness that correlation does not equal causation and that reliable decisions depend on understanding underlying mechanisms. This cultural change takes time but promises profound benefits as it reorients practice toward evidence that truly reflects cause and effect. Building these bridges ensures that causal inference does not remain confined to academic discussions but instead becomes a living discipline that transforms how society understands, evaluates, and acts in the world. The future of the field depends on the strength of these connections, as theory and practice must evolve together to unlock the full potential of causal reasoning.

Chapter Eight

Dealing with Confounding in Observational Studies

Confounding remains one of the central obstacles in drawing valid causal conclusions from observational data. A confounder is a variable that influences both the treatment and the outcome, creating a spurious association that can be mistaken for causation if not properly addressed. The challenge arises because unlike in randomized controlled trials, where randomization balances confounders across groups, observational studies rely on naturally occurring variation, which is often entangled with numerous biases. For example, when studying whether exercise reduces heart disease, factors such as age, socioeconomic status, and pre-existing health conditions may influence both the likelihood of exercising and the risk of developing heart disease. If these are not properly accounted for, the association between exercise and heart disease could be misleading. The first step in dealing with confounding is to recognize its presence. Researchers must identify potential confounders based on domain knowledge, theory, or prior studies. Causal diagrams, particularly directed acyclic graphs, have become essential tools in this process because they allow researchers to visualize relationships between variables and clarify which should be adjusted for to block spurious paths without inadvertently introducing new biases. Once potential confounders are identified, a variety of strategies can be employed to adjust for them. Traditional regression models are widely used, where confounders are included as covariates in the model to control their influence on the outcome. While straightforward, this approach requires strong assumptions, including linearity and no omitted confounders. Violations of these assumptions can undermine causal validity. Propensity score methods provide an alternative by summarizing confounders into a single score representing the probability of receiving treatment given observed characteristics. By matching, stratifying, or weighting based on these scores, researchers attempt to create balance between treated and untreated groups, mimicking the fairness of randomization. These methods have become popular because they separate the process of balancing covariates from outcome modeling, reducing the risk of model dependence. Another approach is instrumental variables, where an external factor influences treatment assignment but not the outcome directly, except through treatment. This method can address hidden confounding but relies on finding valid instruments, which is often difficult in practice. Difference-in-differences methods exploit changes over time, assuming that unobserved confounders remain constant, while synthetic control approaches construct a weighted combination of untreated units to serve as a counterfactual for the treated unit. Each method carries trade-offs. For instance, regression adjustment may fail if confounders are measured poorly, propensity score matching may discard data if overlap between groups is limited, and instrumental variables can produce biased estimates if instruments are weak or invalid. This underlines the importance of robustness checks and sensitivity analysis, where researchers examine whether results hold under varying assumptions or across different methods. Transparency in reporting is equally important, as it allows others to evaluate the plausibility of assumptions and the credibility of conclusions. Advances in machine learning are also contributing to confounding adjustment, particularly in high-dimensional settings where traditional methods struggle. Algorithms such as causal forests and targeted maximum likelihood estimation integrate predictive modeling with causal estimation, allowing for flexible adjustment of complex confounding structures. However, these tools must be applied carefully to avoid overfitting and to ensure interpretability. Ultimately, dealing with confounding is less about finding a perfect method and more about a disciplined process of reasoning, checking, and validating. By combining rigorous methodology, transparent assumptions, and substantive knowledge of the field, researchers can navigate confounding to draw conclusions that are both credible and useful.

Limitations of Observational Data

Observational data are indispensable for studying causal questions that cannot be answered through experiments, yet they come with inherent limitations that demand careful handling. Unlike randomized controlled trials, where the researcher manipulates treatment assignment, observational data reflect natural variation shaped by social, economic, biological, and behavioral factors. This lack of control makes causal inference challenging because the data often carry biases that threaten validity. One limitation is measurement error. Variables in observational datasets are frequently proxies rather than direct measures of the constructs of interest. For example, income may be measured as reported earnings, which can be underreported or inaccurately captured. Health status might be inferred from hospital visits, missing cases where individuals do not seek care. Such errors can distort estimates of causal relationships, especially if the errors are systematic rather than random. Another limitation is selection bias, where the sample observed is not representative of the population of interest. For instance, studying the impact of a new educational program using only participants who volunteered introduces bias if those volunteers differ systematically from nonparticipants. Similarly, using hospital records to study health outcomes omits those who never entered the healthcare system, potentially skewing conclusions. Missing data further complicates analysis, as real-world datasets often contain incomplete information. When missingness is not random but related to variables of interest, simply ignoring missing data can produce biased results. Imputation methods and model-based corrections attempt to address this, but they rely on assumptions that may not hold in practice. Temporal limitations also pose challenges. Observational data often lack precise timing, making it difficult to establish whether causes preceding effects. For example, surveys may record smoking behavior and lung disease status but fail to capture the chronological sequence necessary to establish causality. This temporal ambiguity can undermine confidence in causal claims. Furthermore, unobserved confounding is a constant threat. While researchers can adjust for observed variables, unmeasured factors such as genetic predisposition, cultural norms, or latent behavioral traits may still bias results. This limitation is particularly severe in social sciences, where many relevant factors are inherently difficult to measure. Another challenge is external validity. Observational studies often rely on specific contexts, populations, or datasets, raising questions about whether findings generalize to broader settings. A causal relationship observed in one country, for instance, may not hold in another with different cultural or institutional conditions. The rise of big data introduces both opportunities and limitations.

Large datasets promise statistical power but can amplify biases if not carefully curated. The abundance of variables increases the risk of spurious correlations, where seemingly significant associations arise by chance rather than reflecting true causal links. This problem highlights the need for careful theory-driven analysis, not just reliance on statistical associations. Ethical limitations also arise in observational research. The use of sensitive personal data requires strict safeguards to protect privacy and prevent misuse. As causal inference increasingly informs policy and business decisions, ensuring that analyses respect ethical standards becomes crucial. Despite these limitations, observational data remain invaluable. They allow researchers to address causal questions that experiments cannot, such as the long-term effects of policies or the impacts of rare exposures. The key lies in acknowledging limitations openly, using robust methods to mitigate biases, and triangulating findings with evidence from multiple sources. In doing so, researchers can extract meaningful causal insights while remaining cautious about overinterpretation.

Strategies for Strengthening Causal Claims

Given the challenges of confounding, bias, and data limitations, strengthening causal claims in observational studies requires a disciplined approach that integrates methodological rigor, transparency, and critical reasoning. One central strategy is triangulation, which involves using multiple methods or sources of data to address the same question. If different approaches converge on similar results, confidence in the causal claim increases. For example, combining regression adjustment, instrumental variables, and propensity score methods can reveal whether conclusions are sensitive to methodological choices. When results differ, it prompts deeper reflection about assumptions and potential biases. Sensitivity analysis is another vital strategy. By systematically varying assumptions about unmeasured confounding, missing data, or model specification, researchers can assess how robust their conclusions are to potential violations. For instance, sensitivity analysis can estimate how strong an unmeasured confounder would need to be to overturn the observed effect. Such exercises provide valuable context for interpreting findings, shifting the conversation from whether results are perfectly unbiased to whether they are credible under reasonable assumptions. Pre-registration of analysis plans also strengthens causal claims by reducing the risk of data-driven choices that capitalize on chance. By specifying hypotheses, methods, and outcomes in advance, researchers guard against selective reporting and enhance the credibility of their findings. This practice, common in randomized trials, is increasingly being applied to observational studies as well. Transparency in reporting is equally important. Clear articulation of assumptions, data sources, and analytical decisions allows others to evaluate and replicate studies. Open sharing of data and code, when possible, fosters reproducibility and builds trust in causal claims. Another strategy is to embed causal inference within substantive theory. Rather than treating statistical methods as stand-alone solutions, researchers should ground analyses in theoretical frameworks that clarify mechanisms and guide variable selection. This reduces the risk of spurious findings and enhances the interpretability of results. Natural experiments and quasi-experimental designs also offer powerful ways to strengthen causal claims. By exploiting policy changes, geographic variation, or unexpected shocks, researchers can approximate the conditions of randomization. For example, evaluating the impact of a new law by comparing regions before and after its introduction can provide credible causal evidence if assumptions about parallel trends hold. Advances in computational tools further expand the toolkit. Machine learning methods tailored for causal inference, such as causal forests or targeted maximum likelihood estimation, allow flexible modeling of complex relationships while maintaining focus on causal estimation. These tools help address high-dimensional confounding, though they must be applied carefully to avoid overfitting and ensure interpretability. Collaboration across disciplines enhances causal claims by bringing together methodological expertise and domain knowledge. Statisticians may excel at designing models, but domain experts ensure that variables are meaningful and that assumptions reflect real-world processes. This integration strengthens both the credibility and relevance of findings. Finally, humility is a crucial strategy.

Recognizing that no observational study can achieve the certainty of a randomized trial encourages researchers to frame findings as evidence with degrees of plausibility rather than absolute truth. By combining multiple strategies, acknowledging limitations, and maintaining transparency, researchers can present causal claims that are rigorous, credible, and valuable for decision-making.

Chapter Nine

Applications in Medicine and Public Health

The domain of medicine and public health has long been a fertile ground for causal inference because the central questions in these fields are inherently causal. Physicians want to know whether a treatment leads to recovery, epidemiologists want to determine whether an exposure increases disease risk, and policymakers want to understand whether an intervention improves population outcomes. Randomized controlled trials have traditionally been viewed as the gold standard for establishing causal effects in medicine, but they are often expensive, time-consuming, and ethically limited. Observational studies therefore play an essential role, and causal inference methods offer the tools to extract reliable evidence from such data. The application of causal inference in medicine begins with the need to distinguish between efficacy and effectiveness. Efficacy describes whether a treatment works under ideal, controlled conditions, while effectiveness concerns whether it works in real-world populations where adherence varies and patients present with comorbidities. Observational data such as electronic health records and insurance claims provide insights into effectiveness, but they come with challenges of confounding, measurement error, and missingness. For example, a physician's decision to prescribe a drug may depend on unmeasured patient characteristics that also affect outcomes, creating confounding by indication. Methods like propensity score matching, inverse probability weighting, and instrumental variables have been developed to address these concerns, each with strengths and limitations. In public health, causal inference plays a role in understanding environmental exposures, lifestyle factors, and social determinants of health. For instance, studies on the health impacts of air pollution rely heavily on observational designs because randomized experiments assigning individuals to live in polluted areas are impossible. Researchers therefore use natural experiments, policy changes, and instrumental variables such as wind patterns or industrial shutdowns to approximate causal effects. These methods have produced compelling evidence that even small reductions in particulate matter can significantly reduce mortality, shaping environmental regulations worldwide. Another major area of causal inference in health research is vaccine evaluation. While randomized trials provide initial evidence of efficacy, post-licensure monitoring of vaccine effectiveness requires analyzing large-scale observational data. Causal methods help separate true vaccine effects from confounding due to differences between vaccinated and unvaccinated individuals. During pandemics, this becomes especially urgent, as policymakers must make real-time decisions about vaccine deployment, booster schedules, and prioritization strategies. Causal inference thus becomes not just a scientific pursuit but a tool for saving lives. Beyond methodological challenges, the application of causal inference in medicine and public health raises questions about equity and access. Observational data often reflect systemic inequalities, such as disparities in healthcare access, socioeconomic status, and environmental exposure. If not carefully handled, causal analyses risk reproducing or obscuring these inequalities. For instance, a study might find that a drug appears less effective in marginalized populations, but the true cause may be barriers to consistent access rather than biological differences. Researchers must therefore embed causal inference within a broader framework of social justice and structural awareness. Looking to the future, the integration of genomics, wearable devices, and digital health platforms will expand the scope of observational data in medicine. Causal inference will be essential for disentangling the complex interplay between genetic predisposition, behavioral choices, and environmental factors. Precision medicine, which aims to tailor treatments to individual characteristics, is fundamentally a causal project: it seeks to identify who benefits from what treatment under what circumstances. Observational causal inference, when combined with experimental evidence and mechanistic knowledge, will be a cornerstone of this evolving medical landscape.

Applications in Social Sciences and Economics

The social sciences and economics have long grappled with causal questions because the policies and interventions they study are intended to change outcomes at the level of individuals, communities, or entire economies. Unlike medicine, where randomized trials are relatively more feasible, experiments in economics and social policy are often constrained by ethics, cost, and political feasibility. Observational studies therefore dominate, and causal inference methods have been central to advancing these fields. One of the most influential methodological developments in economics is the difference-in-differences framework, which compares changes in outcomes over time between a treatment group and a control group. This method has been used to evaluate minimum wage laws, education reforms, and labor market policies. For example, studies of minimum wage increases often compare employment trends in states that raised wages with those that did not, assuming that in the absence of the policy, the trends would have been parallel. While powerful, the validity of this approach hinges on the plausibility of the parallel trend's assumption, which has spurred methodological refinements such as synthetic control methods. Another cornerstone of causal inference in social sciences is the instrumental variable approach. In contexts where treatment is endogenous, instruments offer a way to isolate variation that is plausibly exogenous. A classic example is the use of proximity to colleges as an instrument for education to estimate the returns to schooling. However, finding valid instruments remains a major challenge because they must affect outcomes only through the treatment of interest, an assumption that is often difficult to defend empirically. Natural experiments also play a central role in causal inference in social sciences. Events such as policy changes, lottery allocations, or environmental shocks create opportunities to study causal effects without formal randomization. For instance, the draft lottery during the Vietnam War has been used to estimate the causal impact of military service on earnings and health. Similarly, variations in school entry cut-off dates have allowed researchers to study the effects of relative age on educational outcomes. These natural experiments highlight the creativity of social scientists in finding exogenous sources of variation to approximate causal inference. In sociology and political science, causal inference has been applied to questions about inequality, social mobility, and democratic governance. Observational data from censuses, surveys, and administrative sources allow researchers to study how structural factors shape individual trajectories. For example, causal studies have examined how neighborhood environments affect life chances, using methods like propensity score matching and regression discontinuity designs. In political science, causal inference is used to assess the impact of campaign strategies, voter suppression laws, and institutional reforms on electoral outcomes. The rise of big data has opened new frontiers for causal inference in social sciences. Social media platforms, online experiments, and digital administrative data provide vast opportunities for studying human behavior at unprecedented scales. Yet these data come with unique challenges, such as selection bias, measurement error, and ethical concerns around privacy. Causal inference methods are being adapted to handle such complexities, blending traditional econometric tools with machine learning to analyze high-dimensional covariates and heterogeneous effects. Importantly, causal inference in social sciences and economics does not only generate academic knowledge but directly influences policy. Governments and international organizations increasingly demand causal evidence to guide interventions in poverty alleviation, education, health, and governance. Randomized controlled trials in development economics, while influential, cannot answer all questions, especially those requiring long-term or large-scale analysis. Observational causal inference thus complements experimental approaches, offering insights where experiments are infeasible. However, just as in medicine, ethical considerations loom large. Causal analyses can have significant policy implications, and errors can harm vulnerable populations. Overstating causal claims or ignoring limitations risks misallocating resources or enacting harmful policies. Researchers must therefore communicate findings with transparency and humility, emphasizing both the strengths and the uncertainties of their analyses.

Applications in Technology, Business, and Policy Evaluation

The rise of the digital economy has created a vast new arena for causal inference, where businesses, policymakers, and technologists alike seek to understand the effects of interventions in complex, dynamic systems. In technology, the use of A/B testing has become ubiquitous, but observational causal inference is essential for contexts where experiments are impractical or disruptive. For instance, tech companies often want to know how changes in algorithms, interface designs, or recommendation systems affect user engagement. While randomized experiments can test some changes, many real-world decisions rely on observational data due to scale, ethical considerations, or the impossibility of withholding features from certain users. Causal inference offers tools to extract credible insights from these data, helping firms optimize decisions while minimizing unintended consequences. In business more broadly, causal inference is applied to marketing, operations, and finance. Firms want to know whether advertising campaigns increase sales, whether supply chain innovations reduce costs, or whether investment strategies yield sustainable returns. Observational data from customer transactions, loyalty programs, and market trends provide a wealth of information, but without causal methods, firms risk conflating correlation with causation. For example, customers who respond to advertising may already be more inclined to purchase, leading to overestimation of advertising effects. Propensity score matching, regression discontinuity, and causal machine learning methods help firms disentangle true causal impacts from spurious associations, improving strategic decision making. Policy evaluation is another area where causal inference plays a critical role. Governments implement programs to reduce poverty, improve education, enhance public safety, and stimulate economic growth, but they must evaluate whether these programs achieve their intended goals. Randomized policy experiments are rare, so observational methods dominate. For example, causal inference has been used to assess the impact of welfare-to-work programs, charter schools, policing strategies, and tax reforms. These evaluations influence not only national policy but also international development programs supported by organizations such as the World Bank and the United Nations. One of the key challenges in policy evaluation is that programs are often targeted toward populations with the greatest need, creating selection bias. For instance, job training programs may enroll individuals with lower employment prospects, making it appear as though the program reduces employment when in fact the comparison is unfair. Causal methods such as instrumental variables, regression discontinuity, and synthetic controls address these issues, enabling more accurate assessments of policy impact. Technology and business also intersect with policy in the growing field of algorithmic governance. As governments and firms deploy algorithms to allocate resources, monitor behavior, and shape opportunities, understanding the causal impact of these systems becomes essential. For example, predictive policing algorithms may change crime rates not only by directing resources but also by altering citizen behavior and police-community relations. Similarly, recommendation systems shape consumer choices in ways that have aggregate market effects. Causal inference allows stakeholders to move beyond prediction and ask whether these systems achieve their intended social and economic goals. Ethical considerations are again paramount. In technology and business, the misuse of causal claims can mislead consumers, distort markets, or perpetuate inequalities. Firms may be tempted to exaggerate the causal impact of their products or services to attract investors or customers. Policymakers may selectively use causal evidence to justify predetermined agendas. The responsibility of researchers and analysts is therefore not only technical but moral: to ensure that causal claims are valid, transparent, and communicated responsibly. The future promises even greater integration of causal inference into technology, business, and policy evaluation. Advances in artificial intelligence and big data analytics will create more opportunities to study complex systems, but they will also heighten the risks of misinterpretation and misuse. Embedding causal reasoning into organizational decision-making processes, regulatory frameworks, and technological design principles will be essential to ensure that the power of causal inference is harnessed for the public good rather than private exploitation.

Chapter Ten

The evolution of methodological innovations and their implications

The field of causal inference in observational studies is moving rapidly as researchers across disciplines recognize the limitations of correlation and the necessity of establishing causation to inform decision making. Over the past few decades, innovations have emerged that fundamentally reshape how scholars approach data, design studies, and interpret results. Traditional tools like regression analysis and instrumental variables remain important, but they are no longer sufficient on their own to address the complexity of modern data environments. One of the most significant innovations is the rise of machine learning integrated with causal inference. Researchers are now combining predictive algorithms with structural causal models to not only identify associations but also isolate cause and effect in large and complex datasets. Unlike classical approaches that rely heavily on strong assumptions, these methods can flexibly model heterogeneous effects, uncover nonlinear interactions, and handle high-dimensional covariates. However, the challenge lies in balancing flexibility with interpretability because while machine learning excels at prediction, causal inference requires clarity about mechanisms, counterfactuals, and treatment effects. Another key development is the refinement of graphical models and causal diagrams. The language of directed acyclic graphs has become a cornerstone in modern causal reasoning, offering researchers a way to visually encode assumptions, detect potential confounders, and assess the plausibility of causal claims. These graphical tools are increasingly being formalized in software packages and platforms that democratize their use across fields. They allow both novices and experts to think more systematically about which variables should be controlled for, which should be excluded, and how selection bias might distort results. Beyond methodology, the explosion of digital data has shifted the terrain of causal inference. Sources like electronic health records, administrative datasets, social media traces, and sensor-generated data streams provide unprecedented opportunities to study causal relationships in real-world settings. The richness of such data enables fine-grained analysis of treatment effects across subpopulations, but it also introduces concerns about privacy, data quality, and algorithmic fairness. For example, biases embedded in data collection processes can produce misleading causal claims unless carefully addressed. This makes data governance and ethical frameworks essential components of future causal research. The implications of these methodological innovations are profound. Policy makers, businesses, and healthcare practitioners increasingly rely on observational data to guide decisions, especially in contexts where experiments are infeasible, unethical, or too costly. Innovations that enhance the credibility of causal conclusions therefore directly impact public health interventions, economic reforms, environmental regulations, and technological deployment. The evolution of these tools signifies not only academic progress but also a redefinition of evidence itself in applied contexts.

Practical challenges and ethical considerations in real-world applications

As the practice of causal inference expands, practical challenges and ethical dilemmas become central to its responsible application. One recurring challenge is the persistent problem of unmeasured confounding. No matter how advanced methods become, there will always be variables that are unobserved or unobservable but nevertheless influence both the treatment and the outcome. Sensitivity analysis has become an essential tool to address this problem, allowing researchers to estimate how robust their conclusions are to potential confounders. Yet, this technique does not eliminate uncertainty, it merely quantifies it. Decision makers relying on causal studies must therefore cultivate humility in interpreting results and avoid overstating certainty. Another challenge lies in generalizability. Causal effects estimated in one population may not hold in another because of differences in social structures, cultural dynamics, biological predispositions, or institutional settings. Transportability methods and external validity frameworks are being developed to bridge these gaps but applying them correctly requires deep contextual knowledge. For example, a causal relationship discovered in a high-income country may not replicate in a low-income context due to differences in healthcare infrastructure, education systems, or economic opportunities. Without accounting for such heterogeneity, well-intentioned interventions can backfire or produce inequitable outcomes. Ethical considerations also permeate causal inference in observational research. Since much of the data comes from real people living their lives, privacy is a paramount concern. Observational data often contain sensitive personal information, and linking across multiple sources can inadvertently reveal identities even when anonymized. Researchers must balance the value of causal insights with the protection of individual rights, adhering to principles of informed consent, data minimization, and transparency. Beyond privacy, fairness is another ethical dimension. Causal conclusions influence policies that affect resource allocation, healthcare delivery, and legal outcomes. If the methods used are biased, they can reinforce systemic inequalities. For example, predictive policing systems or credit scoring models trained on biased data may perpetuate discrimination under the guise of causality. Ensuring fairness requires not only technical adjustments like reweighting or subgroup analysis but also critical reflection on the broader societal context in which causal claims are deployed. Additionally, the pressure to make causal claims in competitive academic and policy environments can incentivize questionable practices. Researchers may overstate the strength of their identification strategies, downplay sensitivity analyses, or selectively report results. To counter this, a culture of transparency, reproducibility, and open science is needed. Pre-registration of study designs, sharing of code and data where possible, and peer review that scrutinizes assumptions rather than just results are steps toward more ethical causal research. Real-world applications also confront the trade-off between timeliness and rigor. Policymakers often need answers quickly, especially during crises such as pandemics, natural disasters, or financial meltdowns. However, rigorous causal inference takes time to collect data, check assumptions, and conduct robustness checks. Balancing the urgency of decision making with the need for credibility remains one of the most pressing practical dilemmas.

Integrating causal inference into the future of science, policy, and society

Looking ahead, causal inference is poised to reshape not only how we analyze data but also how we think about evidence in science, policy, and society. In the scientific domain, disciplines as diverse as medicine, economics, political science, sociology, and computer science are converging around a shared framework of causal reasoning. This convergence fosters interdisciplinary collaboration and cross-fertilization of methods. For instance, tools developed in epidemiology for handling time-varying exposures are now applied in economics, while machine learning approaches from computer science are being used in healthcare studies. The integration of causal inference across fields promises a more unified scientific language for addressing questions of cause and effect. In policy, causal inference provides a foundation for evidence-based governance. Governments increasingly demand not just descriptive statistics but robust causal claims to justify interventions. From education reforms to welfare programs, causal methods inform the allocation of scarce resources, the evaluation of social programs, and the design of regulatory frameworks. The growing emphasis on causal evidence can elevate public trust in policies, provided that the assumptions and limitations are communicated transparently. However, the politicization of evidence also poses risks, as selective interpretation or misuse of causal studies can serve ideological agendas. Beyond science and policy, society at large stands to be transformed by the causal mindset. Citizens exposed to causal reasoning through media, education, and civic engagement can become more discerning consumers of information, less likely to conflate correlation with causation. A society grounded in causal literacy is better equipped to navigate misinformation, resist manipulation, and make informed personal and collective choices. To realize this vision, education systems must integrate causal thinking into curricula at multiple levels, teaching students not only how to analyze data but also how to critically assess causal claims. The integration of causal inference into the fabric of society also requires attention to technological infrastructure. Open-access databases, user-friendly causal analysis software, and computational resources must be made available to a broader range of researchers, including those in resource-constrained settings. Democratizing access to causal tools ensures that knowledge production is not concentrated in elite institutions but distributed across diverse global contexts. At the same time, international collaborations and data-sharing agreements must be governed by ethical principles that respect sovereignty, protect individuals, and promote equity. The future also holds the possibility of embedding causal inference directly into decision-support systems and artificial intelligence. Imagine healthcare platforms that not only predict disease risks but also identify causal interventions tailored to individual patients, or economic models that not only forecast trends but also simulate the causal impact of policy changes. Integrating causal reasoning into AI can transform predictive systems into prescriptive tools, but this integration must be guided by ethical safeguards to prevent misuse or overreach. Ultimately, the future of causal inference in observational research depends on a balance between ambition and caution. The ambition to push methodological boundaries, harness new data sources, and influence policy and society must be matched by caution in acknowledging uncertainty, respecting ethical boundaries, and preserving human dignity. Causal inference is not a panacea, but when practiced responsibly, it is a powerful tool for unlocking the structures that shape our world and guiding us toward more informed and just outcomes.

www.ingramcontent.com/pod-product-compliance
Lightning Source LLC
Chambersburg PA
CBHW021214250926
51852CB00006B/11
9782205095746